Faces™
of the Southern Tier

Portraits and Profiles of 50 fascinating people.
A reflection of success ~ a celebration of life.

Roger L. Brooks   Elsan Dzudza   Suzanne M. Meredith

J.E.T. Creative Media

265 Main Street, Binghamton, NY 13905 Phone: (800)210-5221

Editor-in-Chief: Roger L. Brooks
Creative Director: Elsan Dzudza

Writers: Roger L. Brooks & Suzanne M. Meredith

Lead Editor: Judy Bedian
Contributing Editors: Roger D. Brooks, Patricia Farrant

Photographer: Roger L. Brooks
Contributing Photographer: Corky Trewin/Seattle Seahawks
Photography Director: Elsan Dzudza

Publisher: J.E.T. Creative Media

Production Coordinator: Elsan Dzudza

Project Coordinator: Roger D. Brooks

All rights reserved. No part of this book may be reproduced in any form or by any electronic or mechanical means, including information storage and retrieval systems, without permission in writing from FACES Publications, LLC, except by a reviewer who may quote brief passages in a review.

Second Edition, Volume I

ISBN 1-891444-16-6

© 2005-2007 FACES PUBLICATIONS, LLC
Printed in the United States of America

A Portion of the proceeds will benefit:
The Vascular Birthmark Foundation
www.birthmark.org

Dedication

Each year that passes I realize how truly blessed Mom and I are to have you in the world. Alexis, you are truly a gift from God, and you will always have the most special place in my heart, from now until the end of time.

Acknowledgements

This project was again the labor of many. Heartfelt thanks to Elsan Dzudza as this project would not have been possible without his efforts; to Judy Bedian for her quick and efficient editing; to Sue Meredith and Tricia Farrant for their continued efforts with the project; to Susan Meisel for her sound and professional advice; to Linda Rozell-Shannon for her contribution to this book and to the contributions she's making with the Vascular Birthmark Foundation; to Seattle Seahawks photographer Corky Trewin for taking the fine photo of Isaiah Kacyvenski; to my Aunt, Mildred Jordan Brooks, who always encouraged me to write; to my sister Stephanie Pirozzi for her input and support; to Raymond Stanton, III for his continued generosity and support; to my parents, Roger and Nancy Brooks, for all that they do each and every day of the year; to my newborn son Roger Louis, II who gives me added strength and inspiration; to my daughter Alexis, who is the true meaning behind FACES; and finally, once again, to my wife Sabrina who is the center of my world – thank you all from the bottom of my heart.

– Roger L. Brooks

Contents

Diana Bendz	18
Frank Berrish	20
Bruce Boyea	22
Anne Boyer Cotten	24
Scotty Brown	26
John Butler	28
Greg Catlin	30
Angela Chen	32
Donald Cole	34
John Covelli	36
Steve Craig	38
Margret "Pokey" Crocker	40
John and Gaetana Crosby	42
Steve Deinhardt	44
Zarni DeWet	46
Kathleen Dwyer	48
Barbara Felton	50
Bill Flynn	52
Alma Fortez	54
John W. Fox	56
Scott Freeman	58
Louie G	60
Dave Gouldin	62
Mike Jones	64
Fred Joyner	66
Isaiah Kacyvenski	68
Danielle Kashou	70
Ellen Kodadek	72
Haden Land	74
Al Libous	76
John Maczko	78
Richard Matsushima	80
Nathaalie Maxwell	82
Randy MacGregor	84
Tom Mitchell	86
Jerry Mollen	88
Paige and Maggie O'Brien	90
Dr. John Perry	92
Dennis Powell	94
Debbie Preston	96
Anne Reyen	98
Monte Pinker and Roseanne Sall	100
John Schultz	102
Tim Schum	104
Pastor Larry Simpson	106
Father James Tormey	108
Niechelle Wade	110
Jennifer Wegmann	112
Albert White	114
Helene Yelverton	116

Forward

I was honored when Roger Brooks contacted me to write a forward for FACES. We talked at length and I knew I had connected with someone who "got it" just as I had "got it" in 1994 when my own daughter was born with a hemangioma on her lip. The concept for FACES evolved from Alexis Brooks' hemangioma, and the Vascular Birthmark Foundation evolved from my daughter, Christine Mary Shannon's hemangioma. Like the Brooks family, I had no knowledge about a vascular birthmark when my daughter was diagnosed in 1994. At the time, there was no internet, no foundation and no books on the subject for parents. I had waited many years for my daughter. Doctors told me I could not have children due to a hormone imbalance. However, I did conceive without medical intervention and that was my first miracle.

Her birth was the greatest joy of my life. Just like the Brooks family, when Christine was a few weeks old she was diagnosed with a hemangioma. I found no support and no information and everyone said "leave it alone"; it will go away. I could not believe nor could I accept that in 1969 a man had landed on the moon and in 1982 the Jarvik artificial heart had been invented, yet doctors could do nothing to help a baby with a benign vascular tumor. I made a vow to God that if He would help me find the right doctor that would make my daughter's lip look normal, I would dedicate my life to this cause. I found that doctor, the same doctor that the Brooks family found, Dr. Milton Waner. In a two-hour outpatient procedure Dr. Waner transformed my daughter from disfigured to "normal." I knew at that moment that the person I would write the book with and start the foundation with was my daughter's surgeon. God kept his part of the deal and now I had to keep my part.

It has been 12 years since my quest to find the cause and cure of hemangiomas and other vascular tumors started. VBF has networked over 25,000 children and adults into medical treatment. Dr. Waner and I wrote the only book for parents on this subject and VBF is now the leading not-for-profit foundation in the world for children and adults affected by a vascular birthmark. We have chapters all over the world.

I found my purpose through my daughter's facial deformity. I am currently working on my PhD. My dissertation will focus on developing the first on-line course in vascular anomalies for primary care physicians. Since they are the first to see the baby, they need to know what they are and what the treatment options are. Currently, this subject is not taught in medical school so there is much confusion and inaccurate diagnoses.

FACES focuses on the depth and beauty of the human face, whether it is perfect or not perfect. It raises awareness that we are all different and unique and whether we have a hemangioma or port wine stain on our face, or a large nose, or if we wear glasses or have any deviation from the normal, we are all God's creation and we are all perfect, just the way we are.

Over 80% of all vascular birthmarks and tumors are on the face. The face is the first thing people see and when a new parent, already overcome with the combination of joy and stress at being a new parent, finds out his or her child has a facial deformity, the added stress is increased exponentially. Most of these parents want to share the joy of their new child and yet they feel they have to preface every introduction with a mini dissertation on the birthmark. This need to defend our child has been evident for centuries and has been researched for the psychosocial effects of having a child with a facial abnormality. The one message from reviewing many of these journals and publications has been the unquestionable unconditional love the parents have for the child. Also, many parents become overprotective of the child, and to some extent the birthmark. Most of the parents, while going through treatment and after treatment has discontinued, will tell you that while the experience was traumatic, they learned a lot about themselves and about the world. Most would not change the experience.

The message from FACES is that we all have one face and every face is unique. The message is also that the mind and heart that go with the face make the complete person, not the face alone. Everyone has a chance to make a difference in this world. At one time or another, we are all given the opportunity to leave our mark. Some will accept this opportunity and some will not. I would not trade a normal lip on my daughter for the 25,000 children and adults we have saved or for the thousands of precious emails from families thanking VBF for its support. I actually thank God for the hemangioma and for the opportunity to make a difference. When I see a child with a birthmark, I see the child first and then the birthmark. In time, I don't see the birthmark, I only see the child. When we look at a face, it is only a matter of time when we begin to talk to the person that we see their heart and see who and what they are. Let's begin to look at people in a different way. Let's see their heart and their gifts before we see their imperfections or even their perfections.

Linda Rozell-Shannon
President/Founder
Vascular Birthmarks Foundation
www.birthmark.org

Vascular Birthmark Foundation President Linda Rozell-Shannon with First Lady Mrs. Laura Bush

Introduction

Welcome to the second edition of *FACES of the Southern Tier*! I am happy to bring the community fifty new FACES. The book is made up of people who do dynamic things and who have shared and demonstrated their abilities throughout our community and beyond. My goal in producing the FACES book is simple. I want to feature and tell the stories of fifty new people each year who contribute to the world in their own special way. Though we showcase the "face" of the people in this book, it is the substance behind the person that I have aimed to share with our readers. In contrasts, *FACES of the Southern Tier* is not only about the "face", but about all the special things behind that face.

Why FACES?

For those of you who are seeing and reading this book for the first time, I'll share with you the true meaning behind the book and the story behind the name that I must tell.

My wife Sabrina and I waited nearly seven years after being married to consider having children. We wanted to know each other inside and out and learn as much as we could about one another before bringing a new life into the world. And more than anything, we didn't want to rush into having a family. We were young when we wed. I was twenty-five and Sabrina was twenty-three. So, we took time to travel, we worked together and we just enjoyed being in each other's company as much and as often as we could. We knew we wanted children some day, but we didn't want to be pressured into parenthood. We even prepared our families early on in our marriage that we would not be trying to have children right away. We told them we would wait until the time was right *for us*. It was also important for both of us that our marriage wouldn't be just like any other marriage; and in-turn when we were ready to start a family we knew we would do things our way, and not the way everyone else did. We both have very strong values, and it meant more to us that we took time to plan our future and our family's future rather than rushing into things. First and foremost, we wanted to be a strong couple who would one day raise a strong family. Fitting in with our friends who had children was important and all, but it was more important that our marriage had a solid base which would transcend into a solid foundation to build our family upon.

When the tragedy of September 11th occurred, it coincided with our timing of being ready to start a family. And like all other Americans, we were struck deeply by the tragic terrorist attacks that killed thousands on that heartrending day. I remember several weeks after the event wanting to go down to ground zero to see the devastation for myself. Although I was nervous about making the trip, I knew it was something I wanted to do and something I had to see for myself. As hard as I knew it would be, I wanted to take it all in. I wanted to feel the dust with my own hands and I wanted to walk on the streets with my own feet. I wanted to one day be able to tell my children about the event and tell them that I went there to see it with my own eyes so I could better explain to them what happened that day.

I was deeply moved when I went to see the devastation for myself. The streets were still lined with photo collages of loved ones lost. The storefronts were still damaged and vacant and there were very few people on the streets. I frequently went to NY for business and had been used to the hustle and bustle of movement on the streets. There was none of that this time. The feeling of death still lurked in the air. I remember staring through a small hole in a piece of black canvas that wrapped around the chain link fence that barricaded the devastating disaster zone when a sudden tear came to my eye. My only thought was that I couldn't believe that what I was looking at was real. I couldn't fathom how so many lives were lost in an instant on one piece of land – all of the talent, all of the leadership and all of the love taken from our world. I knew before I visited ground zero that the world would never be the same, but being there only reinforced those thoughts. It was the most incomprehensible and unforgettable scene that will never be erased from my mind.

No more than a week after I returned from New York, while at home, my wife called me from our upstairs. She stood on the steps with a big smile on her face as she held three pregnancy tests in her hand. All three tests read positive. After being married for six years words did not even need to be expressed. We just hugged each other and my wife broke down in tears of joy. It was now our time to bring a life of our own into the world.

Strangely, I couldn't help but think about September 11th and how new life would begin to replenish the lives of those lost on that tragic day. Sabrina being pregnant made me feel as if we were contributing back to the world in our own special way. Our child was going to be born exactly nine months after September 11th.

Alexis Maria Brooks was born in June 2002. She was very healthy and she had an abundance of hair. The only thing that struck Sabrina was that our daughter had a slight scratch on and above her right eyelid. The doctor told us it looked like a small birthmark and that they were very common; and not to be concerned.

Not more than two weeks later the small birthmark was beginning to grow. We were frantic about what was happening as the lesion almost appeared to grow larger daily and almost right in front of our eyes. We were initially told by Alexis' doctor not to worry, there was nothing that could be done about it and that this birthmark would most likely go away on its own within eight to ten years. My wife and I looked at each other and the expression on our faces was the same. I remember thinking, "did he just say eight to ten years?" We began doing our own research and were told by our family doctor, Dr. John Perry (included in this book p.92), to search for treatment outside of Broome County as this birthmark, now known as a hemangioma, would require intervention from a vascular birthmark specialist. We took Alexis all over to get opinions on what to do as the birthmark continued to grow. We had Alexis christened in October of that year and I remember by then the benign tumor was so large her eye was barely open. We were getting scared and we were getting desperate and we didn't want our first born to lose her eyesight or have any long-term complications.

After talking to many specialists it was decided that Alexis would need to begin aggressive doses of steroids as well as begin having laser surgeries as often as every two months. As hard as it was to make the decision to move forward, it would have been even harder to do nothing. I remember carrying Alexis into the operating room and holding her as they put her to sleep for surgery. I would then have to face my sobbing wife in the waiting room alongside several other families that were there going through the same things we were.

When Alexis approached two years of age she had already had five separate surgeries. About that same time we learned about a doctor at the University Hospital in Arkansas and were ready to make a trip for a consultation. Ironically, the same day I searched for his address and phone number to make an appointment, I came across an article and the headline read: **WORLD RENOWNED EXPERT IN LIFE THREATENING BIRTH DEFORMITIES JOINS BETH ISRAEL MEDICAL CENTER**. I was amazed to say the least. Instead of going to Arkansas, we would make a trip to New York. His name was Dr. Milton Waner and he was considered the foremost authority on treating vascular birthmarks in the world. We needed to visit Dr. Waner.

We made the trip to New York City to Dr. Waner's office and something struck me that day. His waiting room was full of children who had birthmarks as severe or more severe that Alexis'. Some children had multiple birthmarks invading portions of their face and bodies, and I quickly found out that we were not alone. I was very humbled and dazed as I looked around the room. I felt so bad for all these kids, but after a while began to realize that what I observed physically on each of these kids was only superficial. In time I noticed that they were playing, interacting and even arguing just as kids would without birthmarks. That's when it really struck me – these are "regular" kids.

Dr. Waner was wonderful. He came into the observation room to see Alexis and his first words to us were, "I can fix this." I knew right there and then we were in the best place we could possibly be.

Alexis went through two major surgical procedures with Dr. Waner. The outcome was remarkable. He changed the make-up of our daughter's face and the experience changed our lives forever. He changed our daughter's disfigured face permanently by removing the large mass and after only a couple of weeks she would look "normal." He has given thousands of children from all around the globe a new life by braving new medical ground and removing these masses. He takes on the difficult task of removing severe birthmarks that not too many other doctors would even consider removing. He has changed the lives of thousands and has been able to make thousands of children look like "ordinary" kids.

I created this book because I want people to see the beauty in others around them. We may not all be perfect physically, and it is what's underneath the surface that really matters. Whether someone has a birthmark, a handicap, or any physical impediment it should not put that individual at a disadvantage in succeeding at life. If we really try to get to know people for who they are we may find more happiness in our own lives.

I want people to be recognized for who they are and the good that they do. I want people to look beyond the surface of the face. Our society is too caught up with perfection. I wouldn't trade the experience my wife and I went through with our daughter for anything. That imperfection on our daughter's face changed our lives forever and changed how we look at others. In some ways the experience has even helped our daughter become a stronger person, even at her young age.

This book focuses on people who make a difference. I want people to know what is behind the 50 FACES we chose who make a difference in this community and beyond. It does not matter their color, race, age, background, or gender – all people from every corner of this earth can make a difference, and the 50 we chose do just that. I hope the meaning of FACES can go beyond this book and our readers begin to see people around them in a slightly different way. Positive energy is contagious and it goes a long way. Don't be afraid to tell someone you know or encounter that you think they are doing good. Please nominate them for the next edition so we can share their talents to others.

For now, let's celebrate these 50 FACES of the Southern Tier and let's give them this moment in time to shine. That's what FACES is all about.

– Roger L. Brooks

Faces

"Photography records the gamut of feelings written on the human face, the beauty of the earth and skies that man has inherited, and the wealth and confusion man has created. It is a major force in explaining man to man."

Edward Steichen (1879 – 1973)
American Photographer and Painter

faces2007

Diana Bendz
IBM Executive

Diana Bendz has at least one thing in common with what she did when she first started working with IBM back in 1968. She was not afraid to succeed then, nor is she now. Bendz started out as one of the very few women working at that time as a chemical engineer and began developing new solutions for the company. Over the course of her career, she has proven to be a dynamic leader as well as a standout in every division she has become a part of at IBM. She has excelled every step of the way. Today, Bendz is the Senior Location Executive/Director for IBM Global Services in the Endicott Facility which employs more than 1,500 workers.

Bendz also holds numerous patents and belongs to many technology, educational and foundation boards. She finds time in her schedule to also serve the community at various non-profit agencies including being the founder of Southern Tier Opportunity Coalition and a board member of the Greater Binghamton Chamber as well as Roberson Museum and Science Center. Her stellar career and generosity of her time has certainly benefited all those around her. She has had a major impact on the transformation of IBM from a manufacturing to a services and solutions organization.

FACES: What was the IBM culture like when you first joined IBM?

BENDZ: I think I joined IBM when it was probably the best it ever was in terms of its strategic plans and its focus on the employee. That was a direct result of Tom Watson's outlook that if you take care of the employees your business will thrive. I was really lucky, because I joined at a time when IBM was growing at a phenomenal rate creating many opportunities.

FACES: How has IBM Endicott made an impact on the global economy?

BENDZ: Historically, since this was the birthplace of IBM, as Watson and his successors looked to grow IBM, he took this management team from Endicott and actually relocated them and replaced them and left a lot of wisdom here, and so Raleigh, Charlotte, San Jose, Rochester, MN, Burlington, VT – all of these [plants] were really managed in the same style that Endicott was. Therefore, the economic impact of IBM worldwide traces back right here to IBM, Endicott.

faces 2007

"There is something in the air here that's wonderful, and we have certainly made our mark on the world economy in many ways and it's not just IBM, it's the community at large."

The photo of Diana Bendz was taken in the IBM Museum in Endicott, NY.

Frank Berrish
CEO, Visions Federal Credit Union

Visions Federal Credit Union community service entwines with financial services and is the largest locally owned financial institution in Broome County. The CEO who guides the organization and its people to serve and succeed is Frank Berrish. His motto is "People helping People" and he practices what he preaches.

Berrish has redefined the way Visions conducts business and says all twenty branches offer superior customer service, rates and convenience. He emphasizes convenience as being the single most important piece of the business. In addition to his role at the credit union, Berrish is attuned to energy conservation and the use of alternative energies so "America can re-shape itself." Berrish has also been appointed to the Federal Reserve Board as a New York State Representative for the Thrift Institution Advisory Council.

FACES: Why do you insist your credit union go above and beyond the financial component?

BERRISH: We want to do more for the community; we help people. It makes me happy when people come up to me and say, "I got my first student loan from you, I got my first car loan, now I'm getting my house from you." I think that's what credit unions are all about and I'm just very proud to be part of the credit union system.

FACES: We understand that that credit union recently received an award. Tell us about this recognition.

BERRISH: We were selected *Credit Union of the Year* by the National Association of Community Chartered Credit Unions which includes approximately 1,200 credit unions that serve small communities throughout the United States. We have done a tremendous amount of work in the area of helping members of modest means and the underserved, and a great emphasis has been placed on financial literacy. We're doing 240 seminars on premise, on subjects such as how to balance a checking account, how to get a loan, establish and retain good credit, and how to live within a fixed income – so we were recognized for our efforts in helping with financial literacy.

> "We are part of the life of the people in the community and everything we do reflects that responsibility."

The photo of Frank Berrish was taken at the Vision Credit Union main office in Endwell, NY.

faces 2007

Bruce Boyea
Security Mutual Chairman and CEO

With more than 300 employees, Binghamton-based Security Mutual Life Insurance Company of New York is one of downtown Binghamton's largest employers. The Chairman, President and CEO of the company is Bruce W. Boyea. Boyea came to Security Mutual in 1995, was elected President and CEO in 1997, and Chairman of the Board in 1999. Since coming to Security Mutual, Boyea has made many positive changes that have influenced the company's growth.

Boyea's vision for the company includes the success of the Binghamton community as a whole. For example, Security Mutual has taken a leading role in the redevelopment of downtown buildings in a project known as Court Street Redevelopment. This project has recently effected the renovation of the Waldron and Walker buildings. The project also has a vision for refurbishing two additional buildings: the Bern Building and the Binghamton Business Machine Building.

FACES: What about the Binghamton area attracts all of the efforts you have and continue to put forth here?

BOYEA: We have something very unique in the employee base here in Binghamton, and not just at Security Mutual. People here think with their heads and their hearts. They want to make a difference. It's all about the people.

FACES: Why is it important for you to be so involved with the community?

BOYEA: I believe that employers have a responsibility to the communities in which their employees live and work. I am grateful that my wife, Cheryl, also shares my commitment to Binghamton. Her ideas are reflected in the flowers in the planters that hang downtown and the lighting display of our beautiful and historic Security Mutual building. Another project important to me is the "Jim 'Mudcat' Grant All-Star Golf Tournament" for the benefit of the Broome County Urban League. We started this tournament in September 2001 with the help of baseball great Jim "Mudcat" Grant. In September 2006, we completed the fifth annual tournament, where we had thirty-four professional athletes and other celebrities come to town to give of their time and energy for the Urban League. It is a very special thing to see people give of themselves for the good of our community.

faces 2007

"I believe that employers have a responsibility to the communities in which their employees live and work."

The photo of Bruce Boyea was taken at Security Mutual's corporate office in Binghamton, NY.

Anne Boyer Cotten
Design Teacher, BCC
Choral Musician

Broome Community College has had the good fortune of having Anne Boyer Cotten on their staff for the past 29 years, 15 of which she spent teaching in the Alms Building on the campus. The daughter of two musicians, she has thrived in the Binghamton area and in the arts community since she moved here with her first husband in 1962, who took a job with Ansco.

Visual arts, architecture, interior design and music have always been important to Cotten. She remembers vividly sitting underneath her mother's piano as a young child not more than the age of five as her mother played in her magical way or taught piano to her students. Music is so important to her that she started a group of singers in 1978 called the Madrigal Choir of Binghamton. The group is a not-for-profit ensemble dedicated to the art of a cappella choral performance and the choir continues to perform today.

FACES: Who has been the most influential person in your adult life?

BOYER COTTEN: Without a doubt it was my husband Robert Cotten, who had taught here [at BCC] and retired at about the time I started my graduate work at Cornell. Without him I could not have done what I did. He really was a generous, generous man – generous of time and energy which a lot of people have trouble with. It was most fortunate for me that he created an atmosphere where I could go forward and explore the areas of music and design education, and not only explore them, but actually do something with them, and where I was so happy and had been given some gift. He was tremendously important in my life… I was most fortunate.

FACES: What's your advice to parents, and how they can partake in the education of their children?

BOYER COTTEN: Talk to your children, engage them… help them to engage their friends in real conversations. Try to find something that's a passion whether it's something that you're fortunate enough to work at, or something that you do on your time away from work. Try to be more in touch with the natural environment. Be in touch with the world around you. Be able to speak about it, be able to at least ask a question about it. Figure out where the sun comes up in the morning. We're out of touch with the physical and natural world… it horrifies me.

> "A really fine teacher sells their students on being motivated about the subject that they're teaching. If you believe in it enough it's not an act... it's what you really believe, and students, I think, are very sensitive to that."

The photo of Anne Boyer Cotten was taken in front of the Alms Building on the Broome Community College Campus in Binghamton, NY.

faces 2007

Scotty Brown
B-Mets GM

The Eastern League was formed on March 23, 1923 at the Arlington Hotel in Binghamton, NY. The hotel is no longer there, but NYSEG Stadium is located directly across the street from where the Arlington stood. Inside the stadium you'll find Scotty Brown, the General Manager of the Eastern League AA Binghamton Mets, whose entire life has revolved around baseball for as long as he can remember. His father was Public Relations Director for the Baltimore Orioles for thirty-four years and growing up Brown knew nothing else other than baseball. For his career there was nothing he wanted more.

In his first year of management at the age of 22, Brown was quickly promoted to General Manager of the Port St. Lucie team. As a rookie GM the team won the Championship that year. He has been with the Mets organization almost ever since.

FACES: What's the best part of AA baseball for you?

BROWN: Part of the fun about this level, the AA level, is it's really chock-full of more prospects than any other level. There is only one AA team per major league club – so there're 30 AA teams in the country. You really have to rise to the top to even get to this level. When you get to AAA, you have a lot of guys that are coming down in the twilight of their careers trying to get back up, but in AA most guys are still working their way up.

FACES: How difficult is it for young athletes to make it at the professional level?

BROWN: First and foremost have fun. The guys that play at the AA level, they were all the best of the best in their areas. Then they got thrown into this big mixing bowl and all of a sudden they weren't necessarily the best of the best on their team. If they don't have fun – whether they are a reserve player, a front-line guy or deemed a prospect – if they are not having fun this is the worst job in the world for them. So make sure if you are playing to have fun with it. If you find you are the best of the best, work hard at it. Don't let an overly competitive coach ruin the fun for you. If you find out it doesn't work out for you (as an athlete) then there are many opportunities in sports – be it the ESPN's, commentating, front office, sports law, agents – there're a lot of careers out there that can keep your love for sports going.

faces 2007

"This is really a neat town. It's big enough that you can be anonymous when you need to be; but it's small enough that you can get to know the people in the community that can help you be successful and create long lasting friendships".

The photo of Scotty Brown was taken at NYSEG Stadium in Binghamton, NY.

faces2007

Police Chief

John Butler

The Greater Binghamton community has benefited when it comes to safety under the leadership of Police Chief John Butler. Butler has played a large role in law enforcement and has contributed since 1974 when he became a police officer at the Binghamton Police Department. Over the years Butler moved up through the ranks as Sergeant, Lieutenant and Captain before being Chief of Police for a little more than three years. He is currently Police Chief at the Vestal Police Department.

Butler's tough approach has helped combat crime in the area. Many years of being out on the street as well as spending time behind the scenes doing detective work has contributed to solving hundreds of crimes. Vestal, not having the same crime rate as Binghamton, has other issues that Butler finds challenging, starting with the 54 rural square-miles the department covers. He has concerns over the increased use of methamphetamine, the biggest problem narcotic-wise the United States is facing today.

FACES: What single item has affected the increase of crime over the years?

BUTLER: The biggest effect on crime not only in the City of Binghamton or Broome County but nationwide is the increase in narcotics sale and consumption. The narcotics problem really spurs off a lot of run-off type crimes such as burglary, robbery, assaults or even murder. Particularly in the city of Binghamton we saw an increase in narcotics related crime. I think that's the major difference and how you go about combating that is not only through men and women and resources/financing, but more importantly through creativity.

FACES: What led you to seek the position of Police Chief?

BUTLER: There are many law enforcement officers who are interested in rising through the ranks. There are many who are not interested in that whatsoever and simply do a good job from day to day. I feel that both these types of officers are important to have in a police department and no one is more important than the other. Personally, I'm the type who was actively looking to get promoted and you have to put in an awful amount of time and money into studying for these promotional exams – they are all civil service and it's quite an effort of preparation.

faces 2007

"You know that the criminals are going to be creative... they are going to try new things to get around law enforcement so it is very important that law enforcement doesn't stay stagnant and changes appropriately to combat those issues."

The photo of John Butler was taken at Vestal Police Headquarters in Vestal, NY.

faces 2007

Greg Catlin
News Anchor WBNG TV

With aspirations to be a radio disc jockey as a child, Greg Catlin didn't ever think he would become a television news anchor. Things changed in 1979 when he received a telephone call from a college friend offering him a job as a news reporter. Soon after, Greg was offered an opportunity at WBNG-TV in Binghamton and has been with the station ever since – nearly twenty-five years.

Throughout the past quarter-century, Catlin has delivered the news to the people of Broome County and eleven counties beyond and he touches the lives of nearly a million people each weekday. His fair and steady approach has earned him the title of News Director and he not only anchors the 6:00 p.m. news, but is responsible for much of what takes place behind the scenes. He says the half-hour that he is on the air is the easiest part of his day. The real work is leading up to that half-hour in preparation for the news as well as keeping track of the budget and scheduling.

FACES: How does one break into the television industry today?

CATLIN: They've really got to be aggressive. We get dozens and dozens of résumés and tapes in on a regular basis. When I have a job opening at our station, I'm apt to get 200 or more applicants who want that one job. It is very competitive, and it is a tough business – you've got to be aggressive and you have to have something [to offer]. There are so many people that want that job you want, and it's tough to break into the business – you just have to continue to call and stay aggressive.

FACES: The media is often criticized for slanting stories. What are your thoughts on that?

CATLIN: Republicans get mad at us, Democrats get mad at us. Blue collar people get mad at us, white collar people get mad at us – we can't please everyone. Everyday we come in and we don't think, "Oh I have this bias and I want to go do a story and put it on the news" – that's not how it works. It's, "This is a story, people would be interested in this, people need to know this – let's get the information and put it out there." We don't slant stories as people may think. It's not the way it works. Sometimes you can't get one side to tell you something, so the story may seem slanted to the other side because the other side won't talk about it – but we'll always disclose that.

faces 2007

"If you do something that's biased [in TV] people aren't going to watch you – they are just going to switch the channel. Our ratings are through the roof; we must be doing something right. We're giving the viewers the information we know."

The photo of Greg Catlin was taken inside the WBNG-TV studio in Johnson City, NY.

Angela Chen
Pianist, Violinist

Angela Chen turns thirteen on December 15, 2006. At her youthful age she has already reached accomplishments that many adults never aspire to in their lifetime. Chen has received numerous awards in academic honors by excelling in literature, spelling and math competitions statewide. She also performs at very high levels of music while playing the violin and piano. Her performances on these instruments exhibit abilities well beyond her years and her precision and the depth of the music she is able to play are unprecedented. In addition, Chen competes on the Vestal High School varsity women's tennis team as a seventh grader.

Chen's gifted talents do not come without a tremendous amount of hard work and dedication. She practices for hours on end in all facets of academics, sports and music in which she excels. Her determination and will to succeed is uncompromising. Chen started playing piano at the age of four and the violin at the age of six and to this day takes time out each day to practice what she enjoys.

FACES: At this point in your life what aspirations do you have for yourself?

CHEN: Since I have so many things to do I have to be organized and have to know that things are in place. Setting my priorities are important... I have to continue to practice and do my homework. I really don't know what I want to have as a career but I know I want to go in more depth to what I'm doing now. I really haven't thought about the future too much. I know I want to end up among the top of my class in high school.

FACES: You excel in many things. What do you enjoy doing most?

CHEN: On a general standpoint I think tennis is hard to compare to playing piano and violin. With tennis you are out competing with other people and with music you are all by yourself in a room. People may think I like tennis better but when I'm playing piano or violin I get caught up in the music and really enjoy it. But ultimately I really enjoy all three.

> "If people want to reach a goal they have to expect there'll be hard work needed to reach it."

The photo of Angela Chen was taken at her home in Vestal, NY.

faces 2007

Donald Cole
Youth Advocate

Life wasn't always easy for Donald Cole, but he is the perfect example of how we hold our destiny in our own hands. He is one of eleven children and when Cole was eleven years old he and his siblings were taken out of the home and placed with Social Services. When Cole was thirteen he was sent to the Susquehanna Valley Home in Binghamton, where he stayed until he was eighteen. He pursued his dream of going to college and received a degree in computer science, but later decided to change fields. He enjoyed working with people, especially youth, and went on to pursue a master's in Human Development with an emphasis in counseling and education. Coles' love for learning also led him to pursue his certification in school administration. He currently holds the position of Liberty Partnership Program Coordinator through Binghamton University.

Along with Liberty Partnership Program responsibilities, Cole is heavily involved in various school-related activities that support the student body. He coaches the Binghamton High School bowling team and serves as co-coordinator of the Cultural Exploration Program. He is also known for beginning special programs where students can discuss critical issues and learn the importance of community involvement. Cole has a very strong faith in God and says it is this relationship that serves as a foundation for everything he does in life.

FACES: What do you do in your job as a youth advocate?

COLE: My goal as a youth advocate is to coordinate services that will prepare students socially and academically for post-secondary education or a meaningful career. Through counseling, case management and social and cultural enrichment students learn crucial skills that encourage them to become responsible citizens. My job also entails linking parents, the community and the school together in a combined effort to meet the need of each child.

FACES: What is your outlook on the youth of today?

COLE: It's easy to be cynical, but my outlook on youth today is one of great optimism. Children are our most valuable resource and if we don't invest in them, encourage them, and care for them, in spite of what we see in them, they'll never live up to their potential. Every child needs to know that someone believes in his/her ability to achieve.

faces 2007

"I believe that 'Greatness' is rooted in helping others reach their potential, and Martin Luther King sums it up well when he says, 'Everybody can be great because anybody can serve...You only need a heart full of grace. A soul generated by love. And you can be that servant.'"

The photo of Donald Cole was taken at Confluence Park in Binghamton, NY.

faces 2007

John Covelli
Maestro

Few conductors on the world stage today qualify more than John Covelli as a performer of multiple talents and diverse experience. One of the most versatile maestros of his generation and an international prize-winning concert pianist, he enjoys a substantial reputation here and abroad for the many dimensions of a full spectrum career. His musical successes span the worlds of orchestra, solo piano, chamber music, opera, ballet, musical theatre, recordings, arranging, and the multi-faceted realm of pops. In addition to collaborating extensively with world-renowned classical artists, he has performed with a gamut of superstars from Broadway, Hollywood, jazz rock and folk music.

Covelli's conducting career began as a teenage protégé in Pierre Monteux's elite Master Class. Monteux later invited Covelli to be a conducting assistant while the illustrious Maestro was director of the London Symphony Orchestra.

A dynamic interest in contemporary music won him a grant from the Rockefeller Fund for Music as a conductor specializing in American music. During his two-decade tenure as Music Director of the Binghamton Philharmonic he simultaneously served as Principal Conductor of the Glendale Symphony and Music Director of The Greater Palm Beach Symphony, all while enjoying great popularity in a busy schedule of guest conducting throughout the U.S., Europe and Asia.

FACES: What is it like to live a life dedicated to music?

COVELLI: It pleases me that in my case music hasn't been a narrow path. Being an established concert pianist was a great foundation leading to an equal passion for orchestra and conducting which offered endless opportunities to work with great orchestras and soloists everywhere. I see my life as a tree with new musical branches still being created. It was always a special pleasure to conduct from the piano and play over 100 performances of "Rhapsody in Blue" around the country. And I never dreamed I'd be the conductor to premier the first complete stage production of "West Side Story" in France. That 4-year-old at the piano couldn't have imagined all these things!

FACES: What projects are you working on currently?

COVELLI: Of course I continue to play and conduct concerts, and have a huge library of solo piano works waiting to be made into CDs. Also I'm creating an orchestra in the Catskills for young people (ages 18-26) to give them an opportunity which they wouldn't normally get to prepare in the symphony world for the rigors of what that complicated business really is.

faces 2007

"When the phone rings, it could be recording in Moscow, conducting in Singapore, or playing the Warsaw Concerto at Carnegie Hall. Whatever it is you have to be ready. Maintaining a performer's life in music is a continuing challenge."

The photo of John Covelli was taken in his studio in Binghamton, NY.

Steve Craig
News Anchor Channel 34

One of the most familiar faces and voices in the Southern Tier is Steve Craig. His television news programs always give the audience a feeling of confidence as if a personal friend is delivering a message. Growing up in Jamestown he played commercials part-time at a local radio station playing filler commercials during the Buffalo Bills football games.

His career exploded from there in the world of television. He went to SUNY Binghamton in 1972, then started his career at WBNG, went on to Scranton, then Cleveland and finally West Palm before coming back sixteen years ago to the area. Steve spent a great deal of time traveling the world with his wife before they decided to have a family.

FACES: How involved are you in choosing stories that are shown on your newscast?

CRAIG: I choose some but mostly I assist reporters in putting the stories together. It's kind of a coaching position where I help with the writing. I usually advise cutting half the words in each piece to keep it sharp and exactly informative. On Friday I get out of the studio looking for news. This year the focus is the bicentennial of Broome County. It's the most fun part of the job...being out with people and getting the unusual and little known stories.

FACES: Can you give us your view of the changing technology in TV?

CRAIG: One thing we can count on is change. For the next generation there will be no pattern for news. People will rarely sit down at six to spend an hour or so watching the news. I think there will be a blending of the television stations and the web sites where news is available at the convenience of the people at any time.

faces 2007

"I believe responsible use of technology will help us meet the needs of the public. As we adapt, the future will be better for us all."

The photo of Steve Craig was taken inside the WBGH/WIVT studio in Binghamton, NY.

faces 2007
Margaret "Pokey" Crocker
Discovery Center Director

The Discovery Center Children's Museum of Binghamton is run by Margaret "Pokey" Crocker. The museum is a hands-on educational and recreation museum founded to enrich the lives of area children. Crocker was born and raised in Binghamton and went through the Binghamton school system before going to Lake Erie College for Women in Painesville, OH, which her father lovingly referred to as "St. Mags for the Hags." Crocker says she learned an abundance about herself and about life in college.

Tragedy struck Crocker at the young age of twenty-two when her husband died in a carbon monoxide related accident while he was finishing college. They had one child and she was pregnant at the time of her husband's death. Crocker came back to Binghamton after the tragedy where she met her current husband David Crocker whom she married in 1960. The Crockers have two children and the entire family remains very close to this day. Her high energy, her integrity and her love for the arts is the substance behind her.

FACES: How did you get involved running museums?

CROCKER: In 1958 I was a member of the Junior League and my first placement was at Roberson Center. I became a museum guide, a docent, and that was great. I was on the board of directors for Roberson Center for about seven years and a new director came and invited me to become the Volunteer Coordinator. I stepped into that position and I did it for a long time. I then became involved in the educational department and I was with Roberson for twenty-eight years. The only reason I left was to take on a challenge at the Arts Council in Owego. Three years later I got another phone call from the Discovery Center Board... and here I am since 1989.

FACES: How much do you enjoy running the Discovery Center?

CROCKER: It's been a wonderful, wonderful ride... this whole idea. And now we have grown... we have an after-school program; we have an elementary boys chorus that practices and sings here; we have a pre-school that is opening here in September. We do so many fun things... we have summer camps, parent programs – there is no end to what you can do. It was the greatest move I made and it's wonderful to be a part of.

> "I needed to get away from the predictable. I needed to know what I could do. How far could I go? What could I create? How could I do something very different to see how I'd make out?"

The photo of Margaret "Pokey" Crocker was taken at the Discovery Center in Binghamton, NY.

faces2007
John & Gae Crosby
Special Olympics

John and Gaetana (Gae) Crosby have been married for 18 years. They each have dedicated much of their time outside of their work and marriage to various organizations in order to give back to the community. For example, among the many other organizations that they participate in, John serves as a Board of Education member for Owego Apalachin Schools and BOCES and is the chairman for the Mental Retardation and Development Disabilities committee for Tioga County; Gae serves as the president of the Board of the Tioga County Historical Society Museum and is a board member of the Tioga County Youth Bureau.

In all that the couple does apart, there is one common thread that brings them together as the perfect team that they are. Each plays a major role in guiding the Broome-Tioga Special Olympics and their athletes. John is the Special Olympics Area Coordinator and coach and is the glue to the local chapter of Special Olympics. Gae is a Special Olympics coach and secretary to the Special Olympics board. She is often referred to as "John's side-kick." They have both been involved for more than twenty years in this year-round program. More than 600 athletes participate in the local chapter.

FACES: What does Special Olympics provide to your athletes?

JOHN CROSBY: Special Olympics, with year-round training and competition opportunities in over 20 sports, offer people with intellectual disabilities a level playing field where they can reap both the joys and lessons of sports. They can enjoy the camaraderie and thrills of team victory in sports such as soccer, basketball, and volleyball, and develop skills for lifetime recreation in individual sports such as bowling, swimming, cycling, skiing, and bocce. They have the opportunity to learn two basic life lessons that sports teaches so effectively: that practice and dedication are required to improve and excel, and teams can only excel when individuals are willing to subvert their own desires to what is best for the team.

FACES: What is it like working with the Special Olympics athletes?

GAE CROSBY: I often tell people that the more I work with this population of children and adults, the more convinced I become that the good Lord made them right and that the rest of the world with their prejudices, jealousies and pettinesses are the ones with the "intellectual disability." Working with Special Olympics athletes is a very awesome and humbling experience. These individuals are the most influential and powerful teachers of how to work well together and how to love one another...and isn't that what life is all about? We feel privileged to know so many of these individuals — they make us better people.

faces 2007

"Let me win, but if I cannot win, let me be Brave in the attempt."

Special Olympics Athlete's Oath

The photo of John and Gae Crosby was taken at the Special Olympics practice field in Apalachin, NY.

Steve Deinhardt
Coach/Educator

Though Steve Deinhardt hasn't walked the sidelines of the Binghamton High School football field since 2000, he will always be referred to as "coach." With numerous accolades and accomplishments under his arsenal, Coach Deinhardt's hard-nosed yet fair approach has earned him tremendous respect from his colleagues, former players, parents and coaches alike. He admits that he still to this day receives letters from parents thanking him for playing such an important part of their son's lives.

Today Deinhardt applies the same approach he once displayed on the football field in his role as the Assistant Superintendent of Administration. In this key and vital role in the Binghamton school system, he strives to improve the district he has represented for more than thirty years. He manages major capital improvement projects, submits fiscally responsible budgets and works closely with all administrative functions within the district.

FACES: How do you succeed in coaching at such a high level as you did throughout the years?

DEINHARDT: We certainly as a staff put a great deal of effort and initiative into it and we worked extremely hard at being good coaches. We constantly were trying to improve our game in every aspect. From year to year you hope you gain the expertise that will allow you to take your program to the next level. Much of it though has to do with the talent that you have. We were very fortunate for a period of time to have exceptional athletes come through our area.

FACES: What is it about your work that you enjoy?

DEINHARDT: I like this position because you can work with a variety of people in almost every field of education and work to make a difference in their lives and help to make a difference in programs for students... so that's how you affect students. Whether it's getting to build a brand new stadium for student athletes or overseeing the completion of $22.5 million in capital improvements throughout the district, the results benefit our students.

> "You do learn so much aside from the game. You learn about teamwork, you learn about managing your time, you learn about discipline and self-control... in particular how to handle yourself when things aren't going well."

The photo of Steve Deinhardt was taken at the Binghamton City School District offices in Binghamton, NY.

Zarni DeWet
Singer - Artist - Composer

Zarni DeWet, is a student at Johnson City High School who has high hopes and big dreams. And so she should. After moving to the United States from South Africa with her mother and stepfather, DeWet has accomplished more in her years than many people do in a lifetime.

DeWet is an accomplished singer who has planned a career in music. She has a very positive outlook on her music career and has a great sense of achieving success, one step at a time. She is very passionate about singing and composing music and is equally passionate about her classwork and succeeding as a student. She says since moving to the U.S. her views and expressions have been expanded which she is able to express in her music. In addition to music, DeWet enjoys playing tennis for the Johnson City High School team.

FACES: Do you want to continue in music? Just how serious are you?

DEWET: I am waiting for an audition at the Berklee College of Music in Boston. I am not sure what field to go into, but am very serious about music. I want music to be part of my life. I have a CD demo completed and am currently working on an updated one. Music is what I enjoy doing and it comes very natural to me.

FACES: Do you feel as if you have been destined to entertain?

DEWET: It is not easy for me to perform, but it is the only way for me to express what I feel. I get motivated when people respond and associate with my music. Knowing I have touched someone is a great reason to continue in music. When I am performing and the audience responds I am able to feed off their energy and I think I get stronger as I go on. It's a good feeling.

faces 2007

"I have been writing songs since I was twelve and have at least thirty songs finished. I use some [of my originals] when I perform, but sometimes I think in songs and put my experiences in song."

The photo of Zarni Dewet was taken outside her home in Johnson City, NY.

Kathleen Dwyer
Principal, Teacher SCC

Twenty years ago the first lay principal at Seton Catholic High School took over in a temporary capacity. Kathleen Dwyer said she would take the position for one year. However the role was too fulfilling and she continues to guide the school as its leader today. Dwyer taught English for the school prior to taking over as Principal; however she still continues to teach English today and it's something she says she'll never give up.

Dwyer grew up in Rochester and went to Binghamton University prior to interning with Seton Catholic in Endicott. She taught at Seton Catholic Central for thirteen years prior to becoming Principal in 1986. She is very proactive in maintaining very high standards for her students in all forms of education and want the students to succeed at their highest levels.

Dwyer is Board President of the Catholic School Administrators Association of New York State and serves on the Catholic Social Services board for Broome County.

FACES: Have there been many changes in the education system since you first started?

DWYER: There have been many changes. I think private education/Catholic education has gone through many challenges... education in general is certainly challenging, but private education is even more so because we are always looking for financial resources that we just don't have always guaranteed to us. We're faced with issues of enrollment and trying to be better than any school we are competing with. I think we are meeting it and making improvements.

FACES: Is technology helping the youth today in a positive way?

DWYER: The common joke among teachers is when you are trying to use technology in your classroom and it doesn't work ask a student to come up and fix it for you...because the kids know how to do it. I think one of the things that we as educators are really required to do is to make sure that their use of technology is appropriate and responsible. We have a course right now in our theology department on media and morality and some of the issues are use of My Space and those kinds of things on the internet.

> "There are a lot of wonderful things that technology can do, but I'll tell you at the end of the day, there is absolutely no substitute for a gifted and dedicated teacher and a student that really wants to learn... that hasn't changed."

The photo of Kathleen Dwyer was taken at Seton Catholic Central High School in Binghamton, NY.

faces2007

Theo's BBQ

Barbara Felton

On the top of the Theo's menu is printed a statement that sums up the Felton Family: "Family, Faith and a 50-gallon Drum." One of the first things that Barbara Felton will tell you is that religion plays a very important part in her daily life. She transcends that faith and applies it to her family, her business and her volunteer work.

Born in Georgia, Felton is thankful for her strict upbringing. She says her mother was extremely strict and when her father spoke the children would always obey. She knew and felt the love of her parents in the time period she was raised, which she categorizes as very difficult times. Her parents provided and instilled everything that is good in her life including having good work habits. She took those same disciplines and applied them in raising her own family, and building their family business. Barbara is a proud mother of eight children, and co-owner of Theo's for more than fifteen years.

FACES: What about Theo's makes you most proud?

FELTON: Theo's is known throughout New York state. Being here with the universities over a decade, the kids have grown up with us, moved away and whenever they have a homecoming for BU or BCC they come back to Theo's ...that's special to me. We make the food good and healthy. This is so important for the children – they are the future.

FACES: How long have you been in Broome County?

FELTON: We came to Binghamton in 1956 looking for a better life. When my husband sent me a ticket to come to Binghamton I thought I was going to the bright lights of New York City. Coming here was a big surprise, but in a good way. We opened THEO'S in 1991 and Johnson City has been good for us and to us. We love this community.

faces 2007

"Theo's is like Grandma's kitchen, and we serve the young, the old, the professionals and non-professionals... we just cater to everybody – our business is like the United Nations."

The photo of Barbara Felton was taken inside Theo's BBQ Restaurant in Johnson City, NY.

faces 2007

Broadcaster

Bill Flynn

The word polka is synonymous with only one name in the Southern Tier. Although polka is just one small piece of this Pennsylvania native's workload, it has been the cornerstone of his stellar career in radio. Bill Flynn is the "Polka King." He has been a radio personality for his entire career, and anyone who knows him feeds off his high and positive energy.

For over 30 years, his radio shows have pleased all Slavic nationalities which have led to his strong community presence. Flynn is a fixture at virtually every ethnic festival that takes place locally. Although called *The Bill Flynn Show*, the music features selections from all parts of Europe. The growth of his polka show has reached markets outside of the Southern Tier and with the growth of the internet his shows can be heard worldwide at 247polkaheaven.com and polkajammer.com.

Flynn has been the Master Of Ceremonies at many social functions, including the *Two Rivers Ethnic Festival* at the Veterans Arena. He was also selected over twelve twin tier broadcasters to MC President Ronald Reagan's Rally at Ty Cobb Stadium in 1984. The event received regional and national exposure. He is often referred to as "The Polish Leprechaun", "The Irishman with a Polish Heart" but is perhaps best known as "The Polka King."

FACES: How did you ever get involved in doing a polka radio show?

FLYNN: Radio has always been in my blood; I always wanted to be an entertainer – always. While in college I joined the radio club and took a part-time job at a radio station. At that time, in the late 1960's, I worked for a station that played nothing but polka. I needed the money for school so I worked twelve hours each weekend playing polka. That was my introduction to polka music which was good clean fun.

FACES: How has modern technology changed radio broadcasting?

FLYNN: In the old days all of us played records. We had to talk to our audience, do commercials, find the music, cue up the record, put the needle down – that was a lot of work in addition to taking the phone calls and doing the other things. Now here we fast forward thirty years and there're no cassette players, there're no record players – everything is CD and computer. My polka music is in the computer. If someone asks for a song I type in the band and on the screen up comes the song. It is so simple... the technology is incredible and the quality is incredible.

faces 2007

"I really think in broadcasting you are gifted with the voice and the talent... most work is like that. That's your gift from God and that's what you're going to do best."

The photo of Bill Flynn was taken inside the Cool 96 and Cool 100 studio in Binghamton, NY.

Alma Fortez
Jazz Singer

Alma Fortez's whole life has been guided by musical sounds. She has been vocalizing her thoughts and emotions since she was a youngster in North Carolina where she blended her voice with church choirs and school glee clubs. She started out professionally playing in Rochester, and traveled throughout Canada and down to New York City.

Fortez's talent gravitated to a jazz style of singing using the great Ella and Sara as role models. She traveled the country playing at small clubs and then larger venues including the Apollo Theatre in Harlem. In addition, she toured with Billy Ford and the Thunderbirds and played USO tours of bases near Iceland, even warming up before legendary Bob Hope. After the lights go down, Alma says she is most proud of raising her nephew, Hank Shuford, who is currently a University at Albany administrator. Fortez says she has fond memories locally working with the IBM Big Band who performed from 1984-1992 on the lawn during summer months as well as all of her performances with Billy Faster and Dick Depofi at various night clubs.

FACES: What is your favorite song to perform?

FORTEZ: "Someone To Watch Over Me" and "If You Could See Me Now" are the two I love to sing. They both tell a good story and I like to get wrapped up in the musical story. They are the kind of music that never goes out of style and everyone knows them. They are standards.

FACES: Who were some of the biggest stars you toured with and what was it like?

FORTEZ: I have been in show business for fifty years or so...up and down the highway. When I toured with Chuck Berry, Lloyd Price and The Clovers it was like a big family...we always watched out for each other. It was so wonderful being able to perform with people like Buddy Holly and Alan Freed. There is nothing like performing. When I sing I like to bring the audience into my world, to make them feel wonderful and feel what I feel. The audience's applause is like food to me.

> "I've always thought to give the people something to talk about when you leave... that's showbiz."

The photo of Alma Fortez was taken outside her home in Binghamton, NY.

faces2007

John W. Fox — Sports Writer

When John Fox graduated from high school he was very small-framed – only five-foot six-inches and 106 pounds. He loved sports, but didn't have the size to compete so he decided, "if I can't play it, let me write about it." He decided to pursue a journalism curriculum at Syracuse University and quickly became the Assistant Sports Editor at the SU paper. His college was interrupted by the draft in the final months of WWII. Later assigned to 8th Army Public Relations in Yokohama, Japan, his primary job was covering occupation forces' sports, often for the *Stars and Stripes* newspaper.

After discharge, nearing graduation, Fox learned that there was a position open in the sports department at *The Binghamton Press*. It only took one interview. He came down on a Greyhound bus, landed the job, and has made *The Binghamton Press* his home ever since. Today, seven decades later, Fox, while retired, holds the title of sports editor emeritus and writes a column every couple of weeks for the *Press & Sun-Bulletin*.

FACES: Who's the best athlete to ever come out of this area in your years here?

FOX: Locally I think, without much doubt, I'd put it between a Vestal athlete of the early-mid 1960s, Bob Campbell, a four-sport guy who went on to Penn State glory; and King Rice from Binghamton High School in the mid-late 1980s, who went on to play basketball for the University of North Carolina. They are the only two athletes that have ever been the newspaper's Athlete of the Year for three straight years. There may be other one-sport standouts, but they are the two names that come to mind immediately.

FACES: How has the newspaper environment changed over the years?

FOX: I loved evening papers. *The Press* was an evening paper except on Sundays. I enjoyed writing for an evening paper more, but the reason that the evening papers are a dying breed across the country is because people want news instantly today. I loved the fact that if I covered a game at night or even in the afternoon it wasn't going to appear until the next day. You could reflect upon it, form some opinions, do research – you could write a much more polished story and now you are under the gun. If you are a reporter today you may be covering a ballgame that ends at 11:30 p.m. and 11:20 p.m. was your deadline. There's no time for reflection like there used to be.

faces 2007

"I remember covering a World Series game on a Friday afternoon in NY and flying home to walk the sidelines to cover a high school football game... I don't like to have limits on what I write."

The photo of John Fox was taken outside the Press & Sun-Bulletin offices in Vestal, NY.

Scott Freeman
Financial Analyst

Scott Freeman

Some of us in life like to take risks. When it comes to Scott Freeman he has been willing to take risks in many of his endeavors both within and outside of his career. His many years of hard work led him to where he is today at Morgan Stanley, now for nearly twenty years. Today he is a Senior Vice President and Certified Investment Management Analyst primarily working with the corporate pension market and high net-worth clients.

Aside from his career, Freeman has embraced the challenge of climbing mountains. He says the whole idea of planning a major climbing expedition thrills him. He likes that there are so many variables involved with a climb such as the change in altitude, the changes in temperature and the amount of weight to carry. He says the mental training and preparation are by far the toughest challenges he knows.

FACES: How was it starting out when you entered the financial industry?

FREEMAN: I started out as a Financial Advisor with E.F. Hutton back in the mid 1980s and they had one of the best training programs on Wall Street. It was much less competitive back then. The Financial Services industry has become much more homogenized today, with the consumer being able to find similar products along the same distribution channels.

FACES: How long have you been hiking and climbing mountains?

FREEMAN: It really goes back to when I started out as a Boy Scout. My first introduction to the outdoors was as a Boy Scout with hunting, fishing, kayaking, camping, backpacking – all that. As a result, I became more interested in the hiking and backpacking. As my personality matured I was always looking for a bigger challenge and rock climbing became more of a passion because it was more complicated, more involved and there was a certain risk involved that was thrilling to me.

faces 2007

"I've looked at mountain climbing as really a metaphor for life and how I've lived my life. I'm always looking for another challenge... the problem now is I've run out of mountains in the lower 48, and it's no fun to have to look at a lower mountain to climb."

The photo of Scott Freeman was taken at a remote area in Chenango Bridge, NY.

faces2007

Radio Personality

There is calm and often comical voice on the radio that makes people feel there is a friend in the room with them. His name is Louie G and he keeps the audience listening with humor, charm and a vast knowledge of the community. His love for his work can be heard through the radio waves from which he speaks to his listeners each weekday as he delivers his positive outlook on life.

Louie G has been at STAR 105.7 for a dozen years and he says if he has his way he'll one day retire from there. He says the part in radio that was a turning point for him was after September 11, 2001. He says that prior to September 11th radio was fun, but he started to look at life and the community much differently after that day. He knew he wanted to give back and thought the best way to do so was through giving to less fortunate children through a foundation he started, named appropriately, The Louie G Foundation.

FACES: Why did you start the Louie G Foundation?

LOUIE G: I started the Louie G foundation because I wanted a chance to give back. I wanted to provide an opportunity for kids to do things that normally they wouldn't be able to do just because they couldn't afford it... how silly is that? I've always had everything I've wanted and I would hate to see a kid not follow his dream to be a musician or an athlete because he didn't have a stupid glove. I had life pretty good and want to see kids follow their dreams.

FACES: What is something you enjoy doing outside of work?

Louie G: It's probably going to get me in trouble for this but I love to scrapbook. You should ask my listeners. They know me pretty well. I share a lot with them...it's kind of like therapy for me. I also like to play the trumpet for fun; it seems to relax me. I hope to one day play the national anthem at a professional game.

faces 2007

"Talk about having no complaints... it's just been awesome. I grew up, I played sports, I played an instrument, I've had a lot of fun... and the community has been great to me and I wanted a chance to give back."

The photo of Louie G was taken inside the ClearChannel studios in Vestal, NY.

faces 2007

Dave Gouldin
Attorney

Dave Gouldin has had a great deal of consistency in his life. He has lived on Binghamton's West Side for most of his life and has been at the same law firm his entire career. He and his wife Debbie celebrated their 40th anniversary earlier this year. But what makes Gouldin so special is that he is a caring and genuine individual with a heart of gold. One of his fondest childhood memories is playing for the 1957 Binghamton Central High School undefeated football team, because it opened his eyes to the virtues of diversity. After high school, Gouldin went on to Princeton University, where he majored in history. He also continued to play football, graduating in 1963. He finished his formal education at Cornell Law School. After graduating in 1966, he returned to Binghamton, joining the firm of Levene Gouldin & Thompson.

The origins of the firm date back to 1927, when David Levene started practice. Paul Gouldin, Gouldin's father, joined the firm in the early 1940s. Gouldin was the ninth lawyer in the firm when he first became an associate. Gouldin started as a trial attorney, and that continues to be his specialty even to this day. He relishes the competitive environment of the courtroom. Gouldin is very proud of the firm and what it stands for. From talking with him, it is clear he has an extremely high regard for the entire working staff there. Gouldin enjoyed being the managing partner for a five-year stint. He stepped down when he was invited by the Court of Appeals to serve on the Board of Law Examiners, feeling that it would be a good time for the firm to benefit from new leadership perspectives. Gouldin pays tribute to his parents for their integrity and good humor. The community involvement of his Mom and Dad has certainly rubbed off on him.

FACES: Why do you enjoy your work so much?

GOULDIN: The gratification of helping people in difficult times and the camaraderie I enjoy with my own colleagues in the firm and other lawyers in the community are probably the greatest sources of satisfaction. I'm proud to be a lawyer because in this community, like many others, members of the bar step forward to volunteer time to do all kinds of community service. It gives you a good feeling about being a part of the profession. I see it happening in our firm, but I also see it happening with those whom we might view as competitors, as well. The lawyers in this area get along extremely well, and that isn't true in a lot of communities. I believe that civility enables us to better serve our clients and our community.

FACES: What do you enjoy doing outside of work?

GOULDIN: Obviously spending time with our family is at the top of the list. After that, probably volunteer work. I am grateful for the chances I've had to serve on a number of boards and to head up a United Way campaign, but to be honest with you, one of the things that I value most from my community service experience is having had the opportunity to coach teenage boys in Babe Ruth baseball. 1980 was the year that Carl Young first ran for County Executive. I was Carl's campaign manager and I was up to my eyeballs in work that summer. My son Bob came home from tryouts after learning his team didn't have a manager and asked me, "Dad, could you be the manager?" and I said, "Bobby, I'm so busy, there is just no way." Bob countered, "You've got time to be Carl Young's manager... why can't you be mine?" To which my wife Debbie laughed and added her support for Bobby. Eight years later I retired as coach, grateful that Bobby and Debbie had been so persuasive.

> "Coaching kids the same age as my kids helped me to be a better parent. When I was able to get along with their friends my boys realized maybe I wasn't quite as square as they sometimes considered me to be."

The photo of Dave Gouldin was taken at the Levine, Gouldin & Thompson corporate office in Vestal, NY.

Mike Jones
Professional Cyclist

Mike Jones of Binghamton always enjoyed riding bikes. He started riding BMX and then mountain bikes and had a love for riding at a young age. He enjoyed riding all over Broome County with his friends on his summer breaks from school. He raced BMX competitively at Cheri Lindsay Park as well as mountain bikes. He fell away from the sport for a couple of years while in college but quickly realized he missed the sport he loved. After college, Jones started taking cycling more seriously while riding to stay in shape.

In 2000, Jones started showing up for the local Tioga Velo Club races where he was told he had talent. His career in cycling prospered from there and within three years he turned professional. Jones says racing professionally has been a phenomenal experience for him. This year his team did a month-long trip in Europe. The highlight for Jones was being in the Peace Race. The race started in Austria, continued through Czechoslovakia and concluded in Germany. It was an eight day trip that he says he'll never forget.

FACES: How do you reach the level of professional in the sport of cycling?

JONES: When you get recognized by teams and if you are good enough you sign a contract with them, like I did with HealthNet... and a lot of the time it's a one-year, or two-year contract. I had some really good rides in '03 with the West Virginia Cycling Team I was on and in July of that year I signed a contract for '04 and '05 with HealthNet. Then in '05 I extended the contract although next year I'm going to another team. I'm going to the Jelly Belly team... it's a better fit for me. I'll probably be the two or three guy on the list instead of tenth or twelfth.

FACES: What is the perception of the Chris Thater Race out on the cycling trail?

JONES: When I tell people where I'm from they always know the area from the Thater. When I tell them Binghamton they always know it because it is one of the best races. Unfortunately at the end of the year, like our team not being East Coast based, we don't usually come to it. But it's a great race because it has good prize money and it's a good course. Everybody likes a course with a bit of a hill because it makes it harder and more selective. It's a well respected race.

> "Last year we pretty much made history. We may not have even been the strongest team around, but we were the best cohesive team. On and off the bike we were so tight, such good friends and there were absolutely no individuals on the team. That's why we were the best."

The photo of Mike Jones was taken at Recreation Park in Binghamton, NY.

faces2007

Goldsmith

When Fred Joyner was going to Johnson City High School in the late 1970s he was still trying to figure out what he wanted to do with his life. That all changed one day in a class he took with his crafts teacher David Cox. Mr. Cox asked the class if anyone would be interested in learning how to craft jewelry. Thinking it might be an interesting assignment, Joyner thought he would give it a try. From that day on, he would realize many twists of fate that would lead him down a career path to becoming a master goldsmith.

In 1978 Joyner headed to SUNY Oswego where he continued to study and design jewelry. He became the first of eight siblings to have the opportunity to pursue higher education. He eventually transferred to Eastern Kentucky where he caught up with design professor Tim Glotzbock, who coincidently also taught at Oswego. After receiving support from many of his professors, who told him he had a future in designing jewelry, Joyner decided that jewelry was the path for him.

FACES: What did you do after college to pursue your career?

JOYNER: I applied at The Goldsmith, first thing. I thought that Goldsmith would be the only place that I would work if I was going to stay in town. I was willing to move, but I thought I would try [to get in] The Goldsmith first. It had the type of jewelry that I wanted to make, more contemporary, so I applied. I was hired in February of 1985. There were times where I questioned if I was in the right field because I was struggling. Not until we had moved into the Metrocenter and I became increasingly busy did I start to feel more comfortable mainly because our business increased so much and I continued to improve. So I kept on going, but it took years – about eight years to get to the point where I was really comfortable.

FACES: Who influenced you the most in your career as a goldsmith?

JOYNER: Gina [Mowry-McHugh] was the head metalsmith and she was who I really learned from when I started. She's busy running the business now, but back when I started she was the person that helped me and directed me. In addition, all the artists that we carry influence me. Everything that comes into the store you get to pick up and see how it was made; every magazine that we get helps.

faces 2007

"If you put yourself in the right place, everything around you can become an inspiration."

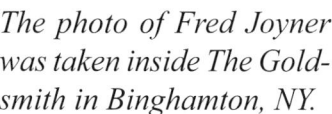

The photo of Fred Joyner was taken inside The Goldsmith in Binghamton, NY.

faces2007

Isaiah Kacyvenski
NFL Football Player

Life can surely change quickly for professional athletes, and for Union Endicott graduate Isaiah Kacyvenski he witnessed this type of change firsthand. After playing more than six seasons with the Seattle Seahawks, Kacyvenski was released in order for the team to make room for a running back due to a starter that went on the injured list. Less than five days later, this resilient fan favorite was listed as a free-agent and picked up by the St. Louis Rams only four games into the 2006 NFL season.

The 2000 Harvard graduate is also the creator of the Maggie Memorial Golf Tournament which raises money for the Wyoming Conference Children's Center. Throughout his life Kacyvenski has always beat the odds, and always on his own terms. If there has ever been someone to overcome great odds and obstacles standing in his or her way it has been Kacyvenski. His mother, Maggie, died in an automobile accident more than ten years ago. She spent twelve years at the children's home where she grew up during a difficult childhood and therefore holds a special meaning to him.

FACES: How do you find the determination to work harder than most everyone around you?

KACYVENSKI: I grew up with nothing and at a young age I realized I wanted more out of life. That became my motivation. By the time I went to high school it all just clicked, and I never wanted to fall short. I didn't want to fail because I wasn't working hard enough. I am motivated every single day to be the very best I can be.

FACES: Why was starting the Maggie Memorial so important to you?

KACYVENSKI: I wanted to honor my mother in some way and give back to the community at the same time. My mom grew up at the orphanage so it just felt right to do something with them. I got in touch with the people there and we came up with the golf tournament idea which was a great way to accomplish what my wife Lauren and I wanted to do. I received a lot of support from family, relatives, teammates and friends. This is something that is very dear and close to my heart and we're looking forward to our next tournament which will be held June 20, 2007 at En-Joie Golf Club.

faces 2007

"Don't regret today because you only have today once."

The photo of Isaiah Kacyvenski was taken at the Seattle Seahawks practice facility in Seattle, WA. Photo by Corky Trewin/Seattle Seahawks.

Danielle Kashou
BHS Tennis Player

Since she was in the fifth grade and had to fill in as her mother's tennis partner, all that Danielle Kashou has wanted to do in her free time is play tennis. Kashou, now sixteen, continues to keep tennis as the top priority in her life. She practices religiously each and every day and would much rather be at the Tennis Center in Binghamton than at the mall or the movies. Her hunger for the sport led her to fulfill her first childhood dream of one day playing tennis at a prep school in order to improve her game so that she could go after her next dream of playing Division I collegiate tennis.

Kashou currently attends and plays tennis for Binghamton High School in the fall and Saddlebrook Preparatory School in Florida in the winter and spring. As a junior, she is striving to graduate from both schools next year. Off the court she is a teenager with a very kind heart. She provides youngsters with free tennis lessons, started a program to help flood victims and even does what she can to help her fellow classmates become better tennis players by teaching them things she learned in prep school. She says her father has been her whole inspiration. She says he is always there for her and provides her with a tremendous amount of encouragement to succeed at whatever she goes after.

FACES: How difficult is the pressure of attending prep school?

KASHOU: I enjoy it very much, but the schedule is intense. Each day we wake up at 6:00 a.m. and start classes at 7:00 for five hours. After lunch we play five hours of tennis and it is competitive tennis. We then have a two-hour workout session at the end of the day. In the short time that I've been there I have really learned to play at a higher level. My goal is to play college tennis so I'm going to work very hard this next year.

FACES: You started your own program to help flood victims. Tell us about this.

KASHOU: Basically I tried starting a fundraiser to help the flood victims but it was difficult organizing what I wanted to do. So I started this other concept with my brother with the money I received from my birthday and confirmation. I buy kitchen utensils, dishes, glasses, silverware and other supplies for the families that lost everything in the flood. I have also started receiving donations from groups such as Lourdes Hospital, so it is growing. When I heard a story of a family that had been separated, each living at a different home until they got their home back, I wanted there to be something at their doorstep when they returned. So I wrap all of these kitchen supplies, my brother finds out when the people are moving back and when they get there they have a nice surprise.

> "All of the coaches said I would never make it in tennis, or even to prep school. I work very hard in order to reach my goals. Putting your mind to something you love really works if you have the heart."

The photo of Danielle Kashou was taken in her home in Binghamton, NY

faces2007

Southern Tier Celebrates CEO

Ellen Kodadek

The Southern Tier has much to celebrate when Ellen Kodadek is at the helm of events such as First Night ® Binghamton, On the Plaza and Binghamton Summer Music Fest. Kodadek is the CEO of Southern Tier Celebrates, a non-profit organization which brings these and additional events to life throughout the year. First Night Binghamton is the single largest attended event held in Binghamton yearly each New Year's Eve.

Kodadek was born in Manhattan and grew up there with her family. She attended City College of NY and the New School for Social Research. After college Kodadek married and had two children. She went on to work for Snug Harbor Cultural Center which is on 83 acres of land with 28 historic buildings on site. She started at the company as Public Relations Director and eventually became Performing Arts Director for the entire complex. In July of 2002 Kodadek became the CEO of Southern Tier Celebrates.

FACES: How did you get involved with such high-impact event planning?

KODADEK: I actually wanted to become a doctor and went to med school at Columbia University in New York before I realized I just couldn't afford to continue. I held many part-time jobs after college and when I worked for Snug Harbor I just sort of fell into something I always had an interest in. I always loved the arts and now I had a career in the arts, and what made it more intriguing was when I took over as Performing Arts Director. From there it was just a natural for me to take the role here [at Southern Tier Celebrates]. It's not always easy being a non-profit, but the rewards are high.

FACES: What can the area expect from STC in the future? Are there any new exciting events planned?

KODADEK: We focus on six main programs and we're continuing to do astonishing things with a very small staff. Sustainability is the most important thing for our organization right now and our goal is to continue to deliver a high artistic product to the community. Our funding is based on our artistic quality and the impact our performances have on the community. We are going to continue to focus on the 6 wonderful programs we have, including First Night, the Summer Music Festival and On the Plaza partnership with Senator Libous; much of our efforts are dedicated to those and the others.

faces 2007

"Our volunteers are amazing in giving of their own time and creativity for the community. None of our programs would be possible without our volunteers... without their crucial work and commitment."

The photo of Ellen Kodadek was taken at the Southern Tier Celebrates office in Binghamton, NY.

Haden Land
Lockheed Martin Director

When you are in the room with Haden Land you can feel the intensity of his presence. Born from an English father and Hispanic mother, Land is the epitome of a model citizen. His passion for his work as Technical Director and Chief Architect for Enterprise and Logistics Solutions at Lockheed Martin reaches globally, and his stellar dedication to his family and community is remarkable.

Mathematics has always played a very important role in Land's life and career. He can recall being interested in math from a very young age. In addition to his career, Haden has been very active in leading the cub scouts program in Vestal. He has been active in planning to help build a new school for girls, St. Peter's School in Kenya, through his affiliation of Our Lady of Sorrows Church. He hopes he and his family can one day visit the school.

He also endowed a scholarship to support student engineering internships in the aerospace and defense industry.

FACES: How important is mathematics for students today?

LAND: Math is foundational to just about anything you do, barring maybe some of the humanity subjects. The ability to problem-solve is a foundational skill in math, be it applied or be it theoretical. I've used that [math] at various levels in my career, much more so in the earlier phases of it; but the core essence of problem-solving is based on math both the indirect and direct application of that. If you're in school, you better be sure that you pay attention to that subject because it will be applied in no matter what domain that you follow.

FACES: What is one of the most interesting programs you work on today?

LAND: Global Transportation Network is essentially the system that monitors all the in transit logistics information for the entire Department of Defense supply chain. So what we are doing in Iraq, what we are doing in Afghanistan, what we are doing in these other countries, we need to get the materials both weaponry, and medical and food to the servicemen and servicewomen of our country. So this system manages that full in-transit visibility of everything.

> **faces 2007**
> "It's easier to work long hours when you know you are helping to save someone's life – in particular those that are protecting you. The drain on me is far less than who I'm doing it for – the effort that they put forth. That's why Lockheed exists."

The photo of Haden Land was taken at Lockheed Martin in Endicott, NY.

Mayor Al Libous
Former Binghamton Mayor

Al Libous always had the notion of taking challenges in his life. After coming home from the NAVY in 1954 he went into business with his father in their neighborhood grocery store, AJ's Market, named after his father Abraham Joseph. He decided to expand the business and stayed with it for over twenty-six years with his brother Bill as a partner.

A close friend frequently asked Libous if he would be interested in politics. Ready to seek another challenge he decided to run for City Council representing the North Side. He was successful, and served on City Council for seven years and as President of Council for one year. Politics and government got into his blood. When Mayor Joseph Esworthy announced he was not going to seek re-election, Libous decided to run for mayor of Binghamton. He won, took office in January 1970, and consequently became the first three-term mayor in the city's history. During his tenure as mayor he also served as President of the New York State Conference of Mayors.

FACES: What was one of your accomplishments as Mayor of Binghamton?

MAYOR LIBOUS: When we pushed for and we succeeded in the welfare merger. Back when I took office former Mayor Esworthy had warned me that the city of Binghamton's costs for welfare was escalating at a rapid pace. I tried several times through the NYS Mayor's Conference to have a NY law passed by the state stating there could only be one welfare department within the county. A bill was eventually passed through the State Senate and Assembly that said there shall be but one welfare unit within any county. We paid our deficit and over a five year period we wiped our debt out and the county took over the welfare department.

FACES: Even though more people lived in the city when you were mayor, has crime increased?

MAYOR LIBOUS: Crime was not a big factor with us for some reason. Back in the 1970s the drug use was marijuana; it was not the cocaine and the hard stuff it is today. We had some crime, some homicides, but not like we see now. I think crime is at a higher level today, in the area, than it was back thirty years ago.

> **faces 2007**
>
> "The biggest tragedy I could recall as Mayor is when we lost our three firefighters at the Rock Bottom Dam... that broke my heart – that was nothing to wake up to."

The photo of Al Libous was taken outside Governmental Plaza in Binghamton, NY.

John Maczko
Developer, Actor, Singer

The city of Binghamton has many hidden gems in the historic brick buildings which line the downtown streets. One of the first pioneers to take on preservation and revitalization of these buildings is John Maczko. For more than two decades, Maczko has acquired and transformed over twenty properties in downtown Binghamton, within four blocks of where he was born in center city. Maczko's renovated buildings are highly sought after commercial and residential spaces. His art deco and industrial designs are cutting edge.

In addition to developing and renovating various projects throughout the community, Maczko also performs as a professional actor. Some of his accomplishments include an appearance on *As the World Turns* for television and *Kiss of the Dragon* on the featured films front. He had the lead role in *Shades of Darkness*, a locally produced film which was released in 2000. Maczko also enjoys singing a cappella and has performed the national anthem at various sporting events such as for the Binghamton Mets and the Binghamton Senators. He has performed with different local bands and worship groups as a vocal lead. He also has his own website located at maczko.com.

FACES: How did you get started in developing real estate?

MACZKO: I got into real estate because I wanted to build a future for myself and a lifetime business for my family. After owning a nightclub for several years and paying rent I decided that being the boss of the business was great, but controlling my future as the building owner would be ideal. From there my real estate acquisitions just took off.

FACES: Can we expect to see more of you on the silver screen in the future?

MACZKO: Absolutely... I'm working on securing my real estate holdings and freeing up my creative energies to be an actor and singer. You can't just pretend to be a singer or an actor. You have to put the time into it if you want to get something back out of it. I am a planner and it's in my plans.

> "No guts no glory! You've got to be in the battle to win it... so step up! Creativity, acting, singing...they're all gifts from God!"

The photo of John Maczko was taken inside a newly renovated loft in downtown Binghamton, NY.

faces 2007

Richard Matsushima
Restauranteur

The Kampai Japanese Restaurant has been a staple on the Vestal Parkway for thirty years. The owner, Richard Matsushima, who was born and raised in Japan, didn't know his path of life would end up in the Southern Tier. After attending college in Japan, Matsushima found a job in the international trade field and did much of his work with South American countries as he spoke fluent Spanish. He set out to move to South America after taking time off to visit more than sixty European cities while in his early twenties. Matsushima never made it to South America. Instead, he ended up in London after losing all of his spending cash and then set out to look for work in New York.

Outside of his restaurant business, Matsushima is very involved in bettering the lives of others through the many organizations he is involved with. He is involved in the local youth-exchange program which sends about fifty students in and out of the Binghamton area to more than twenty countries around the world. His motto is, "How much you gain in your lifetime depends on how much you can give to others."

FACES: What's your philosophy as a business owner after thirty-one years?

MATSUSHIMA: This is a very small community so we heavily depend upon our regular customers. If you disappoint them you don't expect them to come back. You just try to make the customer feel it's worth it. I realized after doing this year after year that I really enjoy making the customer feel good because they deserve it. Everybody is working hard and they choose to come here to spend money. I want them to be happy.

FACES: What are your thoughts on food quality and customer service?

MATSUSHIMA: We have to provide the freshest food possible and we do not want to disappoint the customer. It's not illogical. We made mistakes but we try to correct them. It's very difficult because everyday is a trial. Everyday is a new day so we tell [the employees] to treat the customers like they've come here for the very first time.

faces 2007

"I have interest in people – I like doing things for people – and to be useful. It's very important and it's a good feeling to be useful."

The photo of Richard Matsushima was taken inside Kampai Restaurant in Vestal, NY.

faces2007

Nathaalie Maxwell
Broome County Budget Director

Broome County has been fortunate to have graduates from Binghamton University enter the local workforce upon graduation. The area struck gold when BU graduate Nathaalie Maxwell returned to the area after entering the corporate world. Maxwell was working for Cendant Corporation in their New Jersey office when she received a call from a member of Broome County Executive Barbara Fiala's team recruiting her to come back to Binghamton to join them.

Maxwell was born in Guyana, a country in South America, before moving to Brooklyn at the age of seven to live with her father. She attended Jamaica High School in Queens before going to BU where she received her undergrad and graduate degrees. Maxwell was hired as the deputy budget director for Broome County in 2005 and was promoted to the budget director in 2006. In addition, she leads a dance step-team for girls which she says has had a tremendous impact on her life.

FACES: Were you met with opposition coming into your position being so young?

MAXWELL: I was met with a lot of opposition when I was appointed to this position. Along with being the youngest person, I am also the first minority and the first female, so it was tough. I have been supported 110% by the County Executive and this administration. I have worked with members of this team in different capacities, and I have a skill set that expands beyond finance. I love technology; dance...and I just try to be very well rounded. Also, my background of growing up as a city kid has led to bringing a different voice to the decision-making table. It brings in an outside view. What I found above all else is that people respect hard work. They expect you to do your due-diligence. Once I started and implemented some of my ideas and started to prove myself, people started to accept me, and looked beyond my age.

FACES: How did you start the step-team program?

MAXWELL: I had a friend that was working at the Boys & Girls Club, and I had been going back and forth since I moved back on whether I should start a step-team. So I went down to the club to talk to the director about starting a team and he blew the whistle and asked if there were any girls that wanted to join. Before I knew it, there were thirty girls who signed up. It is a very structured team with girls from ages nine to sixteen. Our very first performance was in the Bicentennial Parade. I could see that this could be a good mentoring program. I knew many of the girls had needs beyond dance, so we implemented a buddy system, and contracts. There is a code of conduct that they must follow to remain on the team. It teaches them focus and discipline.

faces 2007

"I've had teachers; I've had social workers; and I've had parents, who from the inception of this program, have been coming up to me saying that these girls are different girls inside and outside of this program. It's incredibly rewarding."

The photo of Nathaalie Maxwell was taken at the Saratoga Center Gym in Binghamton, NY.

faces 2007

Randy MacGregor
Retired Hockey Pro

Randy MacGregor's father first put him on the ice at the age of three. At the age of four he started playing hockey and as a youngster he learned how to play the game of hockey in a rink in his backyard that his father made. He says he played every waking moment, from the moment he got home from school until he had to go to bed, and wouldn't even take his skates off to eat his dinner.

MacGregor went on to play minor league hockey and always played with and against older players. He was cut from his Bantam Team when he was fourteen, but says he learned how to survive by being the smallest player. He was drafted at sixteen, played junior hockey for a few years and made his first stop in his professional career in Binghamton to play with the Broome Dusters.

MacGregor played seven seasons with the Dusters, three seasons with the Binghamton Whalers and one final season with the Adirondack Red Wings before retiring.

FACES: What was it like playing in the Broome County Arena back in the 1970s and 80s?

MACGREGOR: It was actually just amazing. I am from a small town in Canada, came here, and in the first year the attendance was average. From that point on it really took off and it was like playing in front of a full house every night. The atmosphere was unbelievable and the fans were great, and they followed us everywhere. It was amazing.

FACES: Why did you make Broome County your home after retiring from hockey?

MACGREGOR: You play in a place for so long it becomes your home; it's not like it's away from home anymore – it actually was my home for eleven years. At that time I was only thirty- some years old. That's a third of my life that I spent in Binghamton, so actually it was just like being at home, and I think that's why I stayed.

faces 2007

"Playing hockey, or playing any sport for that matter, there is definitely a high to either scoring a goal, getting into a fight, making a big hit or making a great play – all that's just so fulfilling and it's just amazing to be apart of."

The photo of Randy MacGregor was taken in the locker room at the Broome County Veterans Memorial Arena in Binghamton, NY.

faces 2007

Tom Mitchell
GM, Binghamton Senators

When Tom Mitchell was just fourteen, he left his hometown of Vanderhoof, British Columbia to pursue his dream of playing hockey. He lived out that dream when he was drafted by the Minnesota North Stars and played in their organization for four seasons. Mitchell moved to the Southern Tier after his hockey career ended and eventually bought his own materials handling business known as American Materials Handling & Fabrication Company in 1982. Mitchell couldn't stay away from hockey for too long. In 1985 he became a partner and General Manager of the Binghamton Whalers Hockey Club and eventually the Binghamton Rangers and Hartford Wolf Pack.

This year, he begins his fifth season with the Binghamton Senators and oversees day-to-day operations for the club. His passion for the sport and love of the game transcends into the pulse of this exciting hockey team. If you see Mitchell at a Senators game you may notice that he still keeps his "game face" on even as the General Manager.

FACES: What is it that attracts you so much to this fast-paced sport?

MITCHELL: Ever since I was able to walk I just remember skating all the time, and hockey has always been part of my life as a player and in management. When I think of all the different sports I can't think of a reason why everyone's not crazy about hockey, but I guess that's because that's how I grew up – always surrounded by the sport. If I grew up around baseball or football I'm sure I'd feel the same about those sports.

FACES: Have the new rules of the league had a positive outcome on AHL hockey?

MITCHELL: Absolutely... it has picked up the pace of the game and the skilled players are not held back as they used to be. They can really showcase their skills now and opening the rink has made the game a lot more exciting for the fans and the players alike.

> "In my opinion hockey is the greatest sports because of the speed and the action. It has all the ingredients that spark human emotion... and it's been a way of life for me. Hockey opened up the world for me."

The photo of Tom Mitchell was taken near the players' bench at the Broome County Veterans Memorial Arena in Binghamton, NY.

Jerry Mollen
District Attorney

For Jerry Mollen it was never if he would become an attorney; it was a matter of when. He says he was always one of those boring kids who always knew he wanted to become an attorney. After attending Catholic Central High School, Jerry went on to Binghamton University then George Washington University in Washington, D.C. before coming back to do civil work for the County. In 1980 Patrick Monserrate asked Mollen to join the DA's office and he later went on to work for Pat Mathews as his chief assistant in 1982. In 1987 Mollen was appointed District Attorney of Broome County by then Governor Mario Cuomo and has since gone on to win four elections.

Mollen credits all his experience as a chief assistant for being able to do the job he does today. He says many of the gaps he and his support staff saw in the system going back twenty-plus years enabled him and his team to implement processes to help elevate future challenges. Broome is one of the first counties to have police sign off on video taping statements of suspects in major cases from start to finish.

FACES: What are some of the important things your office stands for?

MOLLEN: One of the most important things that we stand for as an office is fair, competent, non-partisan prosecution. You go to a lot of offices and it's very political. You hire politically, you investigate for political reasons... what we stand for is not something new with me. I was following in other people's footsteps, but I still think that this is one of the most important things our office can stand for. I feel we made the most impact in our work in child abuse prevention and family violence prevention. We've been at the forefront of how to work and try to prevent it before it happens and identify children at risk. We've made some headway, but there's a lot that needs to be done.

FACES: Are the television law shows close to what happens in the real world?

MOLLEN: CSI is ridiculous, CSI is pure fiction, CSI is way off... it's nothing like that. Law and Order is closer. It's not all that accurate sometimes about the legal things in the courtroom, but I think much of it is accurate in terms of the preparation, negotiation and leading up to the courtroom. That's more of what we do.

"When the community sees these horrible crimes it needs to feel justice. I don't think it needs to feel blood vengeance, but at the very least when horrible wrongs are committed there needs to be a confidence that the system is handling it properly."

The photo of Jerry Mollen was taken outside of the Broome County Courthouse in Binghamton, NY.

O'Brien "Chicks"
Magic Paintbrush Project

Jennifer O'Brien of Greene found a way for her daughters, Paige and Maggie, to undergo a special kind of experience for their condition – using paint in the process. The girls, ages four and six, both suffer from cerebral palsy which will challenge them physically their entire lives. "The Magic Paintbrush Project" founded by O'Brien has given the O'Brien Chicks (as they call themselves) an outlet for parents and children alike to have the opportunity to express themselves through painting on large canvases with their entire bodies. O'Brien's husband, Paul O'Brien, does a great deal of support work to make things happen behind the scenes. This is not art therapy; this is a facilitated art-based experience.

The concept has caught on so strongly that many children with special needs and their parents are partaking in this experience. Once the paintings are complete, the large canvases are cut up into small pieces, framed and then sold to raise money from which a portion is used to purchase additional painting supplies. To date, the O'Brien's have helped raise over $26,000, $12,000 of which was donated between the Handicap Children's Association of Southern New York Inc., and the Discovery Center. The remainder of the money went to purchase supplies to help over 200 families paint at various workshops locally.

FACES: How much improvement have you seen in your girls health since they started this project?

JENNIFER O'BRIEN: I've seen the most improvement confidence-wise and the ability for my daughters not to crumble when they have an episode. As an example, Paige was carrying a plate of food from the buffet at the restaurant and the plate fell down. Most kids would fall apart. I looked at her and she said, "That's ok, we can clean it up Mom, life's washable." With Maggie, we have found a way to get longer periods of stretches for her through painting. When she is painting she is able to stretch much better than when she's in therapy.

FACES: Girls... what does this project mean to you?

PAIGE: It means having fun. I like painting with other kids very much. I like to paint with brushes because you don't get too dirty. I like to paint with my feet and my hands too.

MAGGIE: I like the blue paint. I love purple. I paint to stretch.

> "Does painting work? You bet. The benefit for my husband and me is that we're not boxed in; there are always alternatives. We don't talk about what they can't do... we talk about what they can do. When you're always told you can't do something we like to find ways to say you can."
>
> Jennifer O'Brien

The photo of Paige and Maggie O'Brien was taken in their painting studio and gallery at the Oakdale Mall in Johnson City, NY.

Dr. John Perry
Endwell Family Physicians

Family medicine has always been Dr. John Perry's calling. From a very young age he knew that one day he wanted to practice medicine and also knew he wanted to go into family medicine. He says that family medicine attracts him mainly because he looks at individuals in a community sense with the most basic unit in the community being a family. He doesn't think of his patients in a vacuum; he thinks of them as part of their entire family.

Dr. Perry joined Endwell Family Physicians in 1987 and the practice has grown from three doctors beginning in 1976 to where it is today treating nearly 25% of the entire community. He has been practicing family medicine for nineteen years and has enjoyed being part of the growing business citing that at times it can be challenging being so large, but overall the positive aspects far outweighs the negatives.

FACES: Why did you choose to go into family medicine?

Dr. PERRY: I knew probably about fifth or sixth grade that I wanted to do something in science, and probably by seventh grade that I wanted to do something in medicine. I knew strongly enough by my junior year in high school that I wanted to be in family medicine. I was actually in a family medicine program that was a six-year pre-medical/medical program. It was called the Wilkes-Hahnemann Six Year Family Medicine Program. Of the fifteen medical students that I went to undergrad with I think only two or three of us actually went into family medicine. I always knew – and there was never a lot of doubt – that that's what I wanted to do.

FACES: How much does insurance affect care?

Dr. PERRY: Big business... continues to drive society in ways that are beyond our grasp and it has a significant impact and in some ways very positively such as towards what we call "best practices." Unfortunately, there are some ways that are negative. There's talk right now about what's called "paid-for-performance" meaning the patients that are non-compliant for whatever reason, either because they are not medically savvy enough, or because they don't have the drive, you would benefit by not taking care of them... and that's wrong.

"It actually increases your responsibility to the individual by treating them like family. What are the things that motivate me? Absolutely, positively wanting my patients to be treated like family... like I would want my own family treated."

The photo of Dr. John Perry was taken at Endwell Family Physicians in Endwell, NY.

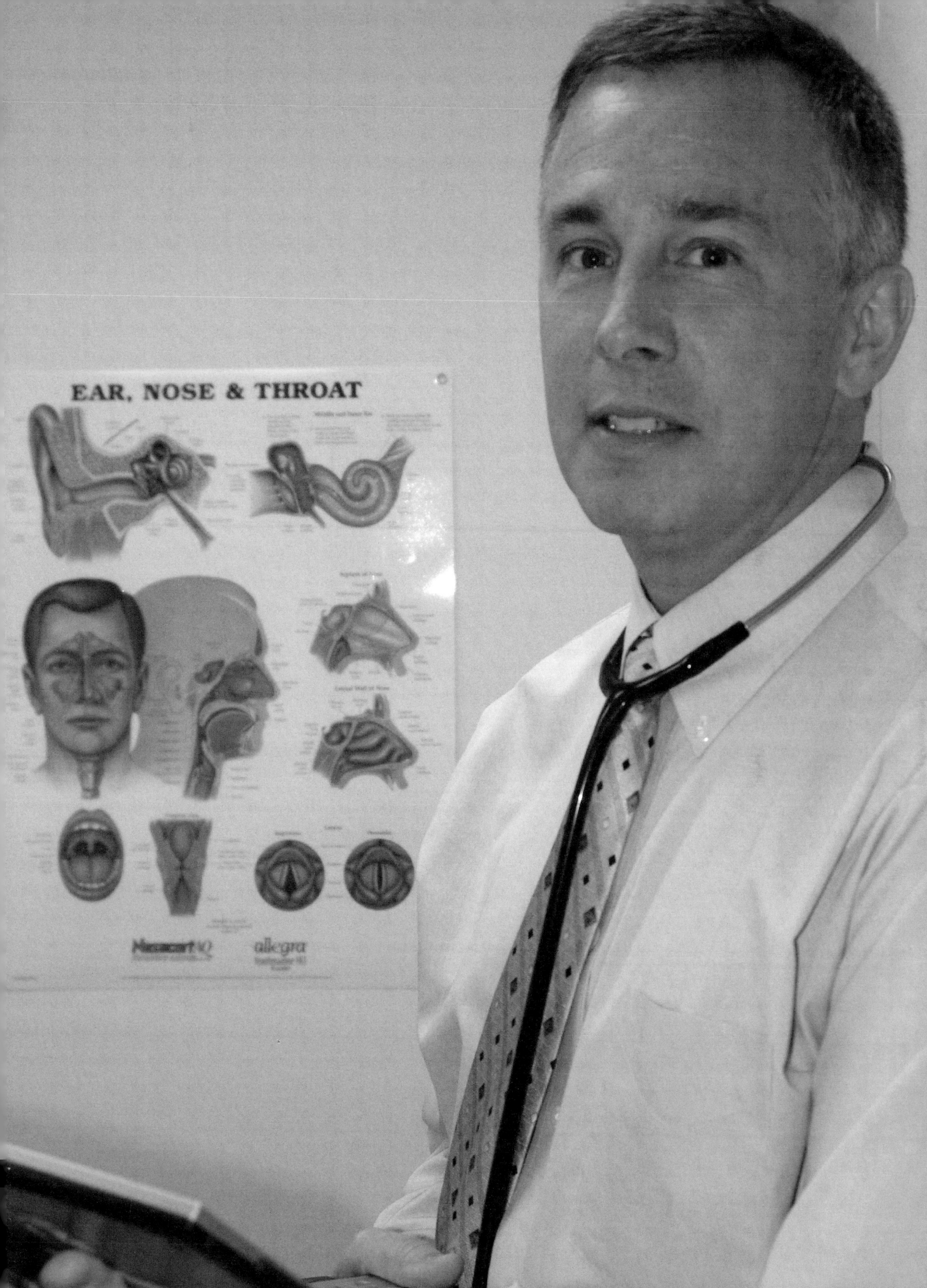

faces2007

Dennis Powell
Vestal HS/ Vocal Music Teacher

Few things reach the heart of mankind faster than beautiful music. For over thirty years Dennis Powell has been teaching young people to make beautiful, joyful sounds – exceptionally excellent, good classic singing. Powell's education included a double major in music performance and teaching, but when presented with a choice he chose the opportunity to work with talented students. His instruction goes beyond the teaching of music as he also intertwines music history and music theory into his classes.

Powell teaches a select group as a vocal music teacher at Vestal high school. Each year he ensembles a talented group of students and each year they attend the New York State Music Association competition. For seventeen years they have had a level six, the highest level choir. The group has been chosen to sing at prestigious locations, such as, Carnegie Hall and the National Cathedral in Washington, DC.

FACES: How did you become involved with music?

POWELL: I stared signing in a church choir around fourth or fifth grade. My father was a singer so it was just something I always heard even though I don't remember much of it. I got really interested in it and when I got to high school I took lessons from a private teacher from the Crane School of Music at Potsdam and that's where I got involved with really good classical singing. When I graduated from high school I was accepted at the Crane School of Music at Potsdam as a music performance major in voice. I had many opportunities there. I sang in many choirs and had opportunities to sing in different opera roles. I worked with Robert Shaw, I worked with Eugene Normandy and I worked with some of the great directors...they would come there and direct us in major works. It was a great environment.

FACES: How do you get your students to perform at such high levels each and every year?

POWELL: We prepare for the best each and every year. It is our tradition to be the best and students chosen know what is expected of them. I depend on the leadership of the kids each year...and there is no mediocrity accepted. I make them work very hard. For this particular group we go back and do music from different years. We go back to Renaissance, we do Baroque, we do classical, we do romantic, and then we do 20th Century and we do some of the tough contemporary music. I basically hand out the music and we go to work.

faces 2007

"Music is alive if we do it really good...we experience the full power of song. We all expect the best of ourselves and each other and go beyond the ordinary and into advanced challenging music."

The photo of Dennis Powell was taken in his music classroom at Vestal High School in Vestal, NY.

faces 2007

Debbie Preston
Town of Conklin Supervisor

Debbie Preston has faced a major disaster in her town and has led the Conklin community with strength and compassion. The great flood of 2006 presented her with challenges most politicians never have to experience. Preston is a native of Conklin and a graduate of Susquehanna Valley High School. In 1994 she attended various Town Board meetings where she began to feel a strong interest in going into public service.

In 1995 there was a vacancy and Preston decided to run for Town Supervisor. She attributes her more than ten years in office to good old-fashioned hard work. Preston also has a full-time position during normal working hours. The Town Supervisor position is technically a part-time job. However, Preston can be found hard at work both early and late at her town hall office diligently working for the people. She says she entered public service in order to give back to the community that had always helped her.

FACES: What's your overall assessment of the flood being that Conklin was hit so hard?

PRESTON: The devastation was massive, but the best news was that there were no fatalities. Our own people volunteered to help before the National Guard arrived. We have 693 homes damaged and 50 businesses. Many people lost everything and it will take years to recover. This was a flood of epic proportions, worse than any previous disaster, and right now I am trying to convince Congress that the minimum amount is not enough to give to people to start their lives over. We need to tell Congress to get out of Capital Hill and see what real people are going through. Right now there is nowhere for residents to return. Conklin will recover and be stronger – even my own home was destroyed. Each night I drive through the town looking for lights on in homes. More lights means more people are coming back...we will build again.

FACES: Are you able to focus on your campaign for re-election?

Preston: It's a matter of priorities. I am focusing on service and getting the government to take preventative measures...I have more important things to do than be involved in a campaign at this time. I care for the people of Conklin and must convince Congress to put more money into disaster aid. What I do is from the heart and I'll do whatever it takes to get the community back on its feet.

faces 2007

"I think things would be better if people were the focus of political service."

The photo of Debbie Preston was taken outside of Conklin Town Hall in Conklin, NY.

Anne Reyen
Community Volunteer

Anne Reyen grew up in Ballston Spa, New York and attended State University of New York at Potsdam where she met her husband Jim who was attending Clarkson University. They married and came to Binghamton in 1967 which has been her home ever since. Reyen is a risk-taker who says it is important to laugh often and even more important to be able to laugh at yourself.

Reyen's first experience with fundraising came at the young age of ten-years-old. In Ballston Spa the Lions Club was raising money to build a village swimming pool for the kids in the area and she wanted to become involved. She put on a backyard circus and raised $15 to go toward the funds needed to build the pool. She says that experience left a lasting impression on her and as she raised her own family while her husband ran Johnson Outdoors she became very involved in the community.

FACES: What are some of the organizations you have helped over the years?

REYEN: I've volunteered for many different organizations and have thoroughly enjoyed mostly fundraising activities for museums, theaters and hospitals. I've done some things for Empire State Games and helped with the founding of First Night Binghamton. It's been a joy, the rewards of volunteering... I think any volunteer will tell you that the rewards far outweigh the work involved.

FACES: What volunteer activity are you most proud of?

REYEN: I'm really proud of several. I worked on the first Safety Town which is a pre-school safety program for children. I helped with the organization of the Discovery Center, the Children's Emergency Foster Care Facility through the Wyoming Conference, Twin Tier Home Health and several programs at Roberson Museum. First Night Binghamton and the United Way's Day of Caring have special places in my heart.

> "I want to make a difference. I want to bring a little joy or happiness to people, and it's led me down this wonderful path with a variety of opportunities to do all these things that can hopefully bring celebration into people's lives."

The photo of Anne Reyen was taken outside her home in Binghamton, NY.

faces 2007

Rosanne & Monty
Rosanne Sall Advertising

Rosanne Sall Pinker and Monty Pinker recently celebrated their twentieth wedding anniversary. What makes this couple so unique is that they have been able to work together harmoniously and effectively to support their clients and the community they have called home for over 30 years.

Rosanne is the President of Rosanne Sall Advertising, a company she began in 1985. Her career in advertising started at HRP Television in New York City. In 1975, she moved to Broome County and joined WBNG-TV, becoming local sales manager. Since starting her own agency, she helped launch Dick's Sporting Goods on its national expansion and has represented dozens of local clients. Rosanne donates much of her time and talent to organizations such as the Binghamton Philharmonic, Binghamton Zoo at Ross Park and many others.

Monty has over thirty years experience in television and media management. He served as president of Gateway Television Group who owned WBNG-TV and several other TV stations, then joined Rosanne at the Agency in 2000 as Managing Partner. Pinker also donates much of his time to the community, serving on the boards of Habitat for Humanity, the Goodwill Theater, the Boys and Girls Club Foundation as well as mentoring students from local schools.

FACES: How has your business affected the lives of the people within our community?

PINKERS: Many of our clients are family-owned and locally-oriented businesses and our efforts hopefully help these businesses grow, and therefore the community benefits. We've nurtured many high-school and college interns who have gone on to successful careers. We also work with our clients and media partners to support events that contribute to the quality of life in the Southern Tier.

FACES: What is it like to be a married couple and working as a team at your agency?

PINKERS: We have a true partnership that has developed over time. We have three children that we raised together in this community and our business is the culmination of a lifetime of working together. We are fortunate to have a great marriage and we learned early on that we have similar values... and that makes it all more rewarding.

faces 2007

"We have varying strengths that complement each other, so we depend on each other to succeed. Once we got underway, there was a chemistry that was remarkable. We could do a better job for our clients together than either of us could have done separately."

The photo of Monte Pinker and Roseanne Sall Pinker was taken outside their office in Binghamton, NY.

John Schultz
Retired NFL Player

John Schultz is one of very few athletes from the Southern Tier to ever make it to the professional level. Playing under Coach Dick Hoover, Schultz had a stellar year as a Vestal High School rookie and scored over 100-Yards in only his second game. He made All-Conference that year and learned at a young age how important it is to be in shape heading into a season. As a senior he became a High School All-American before making a decision to go to prep school in Syracuse for a year. The following year he went to the University of Maryland and went on to have an outstanding collegiate career winning the ACC two years in a row and beating Florida in the Gator Bowl in 1974, 13-0.

Schultz wasn't drafted, but received an invitation from the Denver Broncos to try out for the team. Over a hundred players tried out for the team that year and Schultz made it through all the cuts earning a spot on the Denver Broncos team. Schultz says it was a dream-come-true.

FACES: What was it like to play in the Super Bowl – the most visible game of any sport?

SCHULTZ: In 1978, my second year in the NFL, our team went to New Orleans for Super Bowl XII. My whole family came down and I was chosen to be the captain of special teams. I remember being called out to the 50-yard line with the legendary Red Grange for the coin toss – it was almost surreal. Unfortunately, we weren't in sync the whole game and we proceeded to lose the game. We didn't get any of the breaks, and that's the way the whole game went. Thinking back though, at least I got there. We lost, but at least I was there.

FACES: Other than the Super Bowl, what was your most memorable moment while in the NFL?

SCHULTZ: In my second year we won our first six games of the season and one of the games we won was against Oakland out in Oakland. The Denver franchise had never beaten Oakland – ever. We beat them on an away game and came back to Stapleton and they let us out on the runway and we had to go through the concourse... there were thousands of screaming fans to greet us, patting us on the back – the fans out there were just incredible.

> "I was always really focused on making sure that if I didn't make something it wasn't because I wasn't in shape. I didn't want to use that as an excuse. I didn't want to look back and say – if I would have only done it."

The photo of John Schultz was taken inside his office in Vestal, NY.

Tim Schum
Soccer Aficionado

If you mention the word soccer at Binghamton University or anywhere in Broome County for that matter, it is synonymous with the name Tim Schum. From 1963-1992, Schum coached the game of soccer at Binghamton University and amassed a 259-126-43 record while making sixteen post-season tournament appearances, including two ECAC Championships and six SUNY Athletic Conference Titles. He has also been involved with numerous soccer tournaments and has served the National Soccer Coaches Association of America on various levels since 1978, including serving as president in 1982-83.

Schum has also compiled countless awards in the soccer arena including being selected to the National Soccer Hall of Fame in August of 2004 and the Binghamton University Sports Hall of Fame in 1999. His love for the sport and instruction of the game is truly a devotion not many can share. Schum is the author of a book coming out in the spring of 2007 called *From Colonials to Bearcats, A History of Binghamton University Athletics 1946-2006* which will surely be an interesting read.

FACES: How did you get involved with soccer to begin with?

SCHUM: My dad was a high school athletic coach in Spencerport, NY for soccer, basketball and baseball. The school was not big enough to have a football team so soccer was the fall sport. The city of Rochester had many immigrants from many different parts of the world when I was growing up and that helped the sport. I grew up riding the bus with my dad for all the road games and was constantly surrounded by sports. I played four years of high school soccer and then four years at the University of Rochester before coming to this area...so it has always been part of my life. It opened a great deal of opportunity for me.

FACES: Do you think soccer will get to a higher level in the US in order to compete with many great teams around the globe?

SCHUM: It has happened in a sense. Our team didn't do very well this year at the World Cup level, but in 2002 we had a very good run and we really outplayed Germany, only to lose in the quarter-finals. We have gained a lot of acceptance internationally. My wife's family is from Argentina and one year when the US team beat Argentina – you can imagine the e-mails we received. The point is there is knowledge around the world that the US is making quality improvement in the sport. It has been slow growth but we are making strides.

> "Soccer's next vital US initiative will be to develop an enhanced culture for the sport in this country. Included will be a need to have the thousands of players and supporters be more productive in supporting the sports outside of their own locales. If this occurs, I predict greater US appreciation for soccer including increased support for media coverage and the professional game."

The photo of Tim Schum was taken on the soccer practice field at Binghamton University in Vestal, NY.

Pastor Larry Simpson
New Heights Ministries

Larry Simpson

Pastor Larry Simpson was born in Douglass, Georgia and as a toddler he moved to Elmira, NY with his family. He says he lived a very normal childhood involved with many activities but it was the church that gave him a balance. He was born and raised in the church and is grateful to his parents for such a wonderful and sound upbringing.

After a career at IBM Endicott in the Human Resource Department, Pastor Simpson decided to pursue his dream of one day having a church of his own. He decided to go into the ministry and become a pastor. Religion had played a very important role in Pastor Simpson's upbringing as his mother is one of nineteen children and the entire family is religious. Today, his wife and son are very involved with his church called New Heights Ministries which opened its doors at their new building this year.

FACES: What caused you to want to work with people as a Pastor?

PASTOR SIMPSON: It's not just black people or white people, but it's all people. It's not just old people or young people, but it's everybody in between. It's not just the rich or the poor, it's everyone in between because the rich can have problems just like the poor can have problems. So God and the love of people is what keeps me going.

FACES: How has the family structure changed since when you grew up?

PASTOR SIMPSON: I grew up in a family structure where there was a mom and a dad at home. Unfortunately, right now you find a lot of single-family homes...a lot of children who grow up with just the moms and the dads are missing. There are not the same family values and many of the kids nowadays do not go to church. When I grew up we went to church as a family, we came home as a family, we would eat dinner as a family and we would go on vacation as a family. I think this is what we have lost today and that's why the church is there.

faces 2007

"My love for God and my love for people drive me. I love people and I want to see people healed both physically and emotionally and spiritually. I want to see people delivered from whatever their struggles are...and I just want to see people set free."

The photo of Pastor Larry Simpson was taken outside New Heights Ministries Church in Binghamton, NY.

Father James Tormey
Catholic Priest

Father James Tormey is the product of twenty-one years of Catholic education at a time he describes as "a different era then." The son of the captain of the fire department from Rome, NY, he went on to the seminary in 1971 and made his parents and family very proud. He spent eight years in the seminary and his first eight years as an ordained priest in Syracuse before being called to Binghamton to become the chaplain at Lourdes Hospital in 1988.

In 1995 Father Tormey was assigned to St. Thomas Aquinas Church by Bishop Joseph T. O'Keefe. He has been committed to serving this community and his congregation since then. His schedule is non-stop as he oversees every aspect of running a church. His passion outside of his church responsibilities is playing classical piano, and mainly the works of Chopin. Father Tormey hopes to one day take time out and act as a chaplain and piano player and circumnavigate the globe on a cruise ship.

FACES: How do we educate our children about the importance of religion?

FATHER TORMEY: It has to start from home. Children mimic their parents; they are going to mimic what they see. I think that parents today are becoming more involved in their children's lives and are taking a keen interest in their children's development – even more so than of my parents' era. The young parents today, I'm very heartened to see, are very committed and really want to get involved in every aspect of their children's lives.

FACES: What are your thoughts about the consolidation of churches today?

FATHER TORMEY: The thing about bringing parishes together – as tragic and sad as it is for people who have such an investment in these buildings and communities – is that it's going to create a much larger, dynamic faith community where a lot of people with a lot of different gifts will be able to come together. This will happen once everything settles and the hurt feelings are gone, because you can't minimize the hurt feelings.

"If religion is authentic, and if it's pure, and if it's true, it can be a healing bond and a source of peace for the world, and can call us to our better selves."

The photo of Father James Tormey was taken inside the rectory at St. Thomas Aquinas Church in Binghamton, NY.

faces2007

Niechelle Wade
Organic Farmer

Niechelle Wade enjoyed going to her grandparents farm as a child. As she grew up she became more and more intrigued with the farm and the many aspects of running it as a business. When opportunity presented itself for Wade to take over the family farm she couldn't refuse. The farm has now been in the family for seven generations and sits on 160 acres just south of Whitney Point. Wade and her family raise certified organic produce as well as pastured beef and pork.

In addition to operating the family business, Wade is also very active in the community volunteering her scare free time supporting and educating the community about the benefits of agriculture and healthy eating. She is the president of the Susquenango Chapter of the Northeast Organic Farming Association, she manages the Johnson City and Whitney Point Farmers Markets, and she serves on the committee for the Binghamton Farmers Market. In addition, she serves on the board of directors for Cornell University Cooperative Extension of Broome County.

FACES: How can we utilize the farmland that we have in our area as an asset to the community?

WADE: My vision is to revitalize our regional identity starting with our strong agricultural heritage and working up from there. I believe that organizing and packaging all these assets and touting them to the tourist population could be one of the answers to revitalizing our community as it is, not by trying to become something else.

FACES: What are some of the things you are doing in the community with your farming?

WADE: We do the Farm Days at the Oakdale Mall. It's now our third year and turnout is tremendous. They get more people coming in for Farm Days than they do on Black Friday. You see people for the most part when it's the only time they get to interact with live animals. You see their interest and it's nice being able to educate them because that is what I like to do most. It's the same with the farmers markets and I found a really good niche for myself educating people about food and not being afraid of being obsessed with fat grams and counting every calorie. My dream is to turn my house into a seasonal restaurant to have control over the raw ingredients that I cook with. All my years waiting tables and learning to deal with people, plus my knowledge of food...I would enjoy running a restaurant.

faces 2007

"Our next step is to try to get a year-round venue because the farmers markets close in October. The customers want something in the winter so we are going to try to figure a way to get this done."

The photo of Niechelle Wade was taken outside her farm in Whitney Point, NY.

faces2007

Jen Wegmann
Binghamton University

Jennifer Wegmann's positive attitude and competitive nature has kept her on top of her game both in her professional life and as a former collegiate basketball standout. Wegmann received a full scholarship from Division I Iona College after attending Windsor High School. After two years she decided she wanted to come home to finish out her college career after having some injuries and difference in philosophy. She enjoyed playing at Division III Binghamton as the team's Center for two years.

She is currently a lecturer at Binghamton University teaching six different classes: two classes in nutrition, women's wellness, wellness through aerobics, a body-toning class and the class she is most proud of called Love Thy Self. The class focuses on women learning to love and respect and accept their bodies. Wegmann designed the Women's Wellness and Love Thy Self class.

FACES: How did you begin the Love Thy Self course?

WEGMANN: When I was working on my thesis for my masters, my project was the Socialization of the Patriarchal System & the Delivery of Women in Health Care. What I looked at was how the medical system had been socialized to behave in a patriarchal manner towards women when they go to get their healthcare… so, for example, I'm the Dad and you do what I say. What I found in that research is that the more women knew about their bodies the more empowered they were when going to the doctor. If they had a question they would be more assertive to talk about their question. So that's where the class came from and I thought if I could get a group of women together and teach them about themselves they would be more assertive and take more responsibility for their own health.

FACES: How tough is the pressure today for student athletes?

WEGMANN: I think the amount of focus they put on weight training to gain that strength and muscle mass is much different than it was ten or fifteen years ago. I think the pressure varies by coach, by school, by team… I have definitely seen a lot of men and women who have had issues related to athletics. I know myself the pressure I was put under as an athlete… it was one of the biggest reasons why I left Iona - my coach kept telling me I was fat.

faces 2007

"I'm trying to change the mindset of what the media portrays as to what women should look like. They're bombarded with pictures of a standard that society set up that's really unattainable for most women… and they can't escape it."

The photo of Jennifer Wegmann was taken inside the Binghamton University Events Center in Vestal, NY.

Albert White
Artist

Albert White, a Mohawk Indian, has been following the traditions of recording and sharing the history of his people all his life. Born in Binghamton he attended San Francisco Art Institute and graduated with honors from the Maryland Institute of Art. In 1975 he joined the American Indian Movement. Through this involvement he has seen and preserved, in paintings and memories, the struggles resulting in the resurgence of Native American-Indian pride and prominence.

As an artist White's paintings reflect sensitivity and power in wildlife, people and the land. His art work has been shown in venues across the country and is in the permanent collections of major institutions. He has served as an exhibitor, lecturer and teacher in many prestigious locations, and is currently a teacher at The Art School located in Broome County.

FACES: Were there any people who gave you special inspiration?

ALBERT: Yes, two teachers, one at the college level and another in post-graduate school taught me a lot. They taught me practical things like how to create my own paints and each stressed always striving to be better...in whatever endeavor I am involved with.

FACES: Do you have many interests outside your art?

ALBERT: I love music and have a great appreciation for jazz. Animals are also important to me. I own horses and a special dog. If a god wanted to punish the world all he would have to do is take away all the animals.

"The Friendship Dance is a continual circle that moves in one direction and then reverses. Like life, as soon as you think you know a lot, something changes, and the reverses teach those who pay attention."

The photo of of Albert White was taken inside the Bundy Museum in Binghamton, NY.

faces 2007

Helene Yelverton
Teacher, Choreographer, Studio Owner

Helene Yelverton

Life can be a 'walk in the park'. Just ask Helene Yelverton who has been able to very successfully 'dance her way through life'. Performer; Teacher; Choreographer; and Inspiration to hundreds of aspiring young people – all describe Yelverton. She has been dancing since age eight and opened her own Studio at the tender age of seventeen back in 1959. Under the tutelage of famed teacher/director Helen Foley, Yelverton auditioned for and was accepted by the School of American Ballet in New York City. She began her career under the watchful eye of famed Ballet Guru, George Balanchine. Over the years, Helene has spent much time in NYC; Training, Teaching, Judging and watching a large number of former students perform on Broadway.

Yelverton's early career began as Endicott Johnson's 'Dancing Star' at age twelve. She performed with EJ's Orchestra, under the direction of Mr. Frank Tae at company banquets and special events. Yelverton says, "That early experience most probably contributed to my felling very comfortable choreographing for and performing on stage in front of large groups."

FACES: Have there been any 'stand out' students from your school?

Yelverton: Oh yes, a good number. For example, Melanie Gage performed on Broadway, TV, Motion Pictures (she was in the Movie "Chicago" and choreographed "Beyond the Sea"). Another former student, Greg Daniels (Voutsinas) has been dancing and choreographing professionally for 24 years and currently is in the *Radio City Christmas Spectacular*. Actually, I had five former students dancing professionally on stages in Las Vegas all at the same time just a couple of years ago. I also have had a significant number of kids go on to college, major in dance, and then open their own schools (5 in this area alone). But please understand, I'm just as proud of the thousands (over 10,000 during the past 47 years) of young people who have gone on to become productive, well adjusted and happy adults, now raising their own children. I have many of their children; second and third generation students, at my school.

FACES: What are your plans now after 47 years in Business?

Yelverton: My family would like to see me slow down and 'smell the flowers' (we have a new home in Florida), but quite honestly, my flowers are right here in this Studio. I guess I'll continue doing what I do as long as God favors me with good health, the kids continue to benefit, and 'the river don't rise' (again).

faces 2007

"I love to dance... dance is love."

The photo of Helene Yelverton was taken inside her dance studio in Conklin, NY.

Faces

authors 2007

Roger L. Brooks
Editor-in-Chief

Roger L. Brooks, 37, is the Editor-in-Chief and founder of FACES Publications, LLC. He embarked on this venture in the spring of 2005 for the first edition of *FACES of the Southern Tier*. Brooks was the lead author and photographer for this edition. He plans to produce the publication annually in the Southern Tier as well as expand the concept beyond the local area. He is currently finalizing a new book *My Daughter's Face, Her Precious Face* which is scheduled to be released in the spring of 2007. The book is a memoir and account of his experience in dealing with a child born with a hemangioma (benign vascular tumor).

Brooks was born and raised in Binghamton, NY. He attended Binghamton High School and Broome Community College before transferring to Portland State University in Portland, Oregon in 1990. While in college he started an apparel company, RIP City T's, and produced clothing for retailers throughout the Pacific Northwest.

In Portland, Brooks partnered with NBA legend Clyde Drexler and in 1992 formed Slamma Jamma Sports, which produced a product line of apparel for Mr. Drexler. From 1993-1999, he worked for Binghamton based Dine-A-Mate, Inc. where he was responsible for bringing the Dine-A-Mate product to the West Coast. He played a key role in the expansion of Dine-A-Mate which was listed in *Inc. Magazine* as one of the fastest growing private companies in America from 1994-1997, respectfully. He returned to Binghamton in 1996 to work at the company's corporate office.

Brooks is involved with multiple business ventures including working for ValueCentric Marketing Group of Binghamton which produces loyalty and rewards programs internationally to large retailers, banks, credit card companies and gas and convenient stores. He serves the community on various boards including the Zoning Board of Appeals for the city of Binghamton, the Boys & Girls Club Foundation and the Binghamton Zoo at Ross Park. He resides in Binghamton with his wife Sabrina, their daughter Alexis and son Roger, II.

Elsan Dzudza
Creative Director

One of the new generation web artists, Elsan Dzudza has been actively involved in the graphic/web industry for more than 10 years. His clients range from individuals and small private businesses to Fortune 500 companies. Dzudza has been exploring many new and unconventional ways to capture an audience's attention and to get his client's message across.

Dzudza's passion for art and design was evident from an early age. His father was a well-known European architect. "While I 'inherited' passion for art from my Mom, I learned the craft from my Dad. I started sketching and drawing by his side very early while he was working on architectural drawings. It was all very exciting." Very soon Dzudza was helping his father with project ideas and concepts. He was influenced by the works of Leonardo Da Vinci, LeCorbusier and Frank Lloyd Wright. Throughout high school and later in college Dzudza was consumed with the idea of exploring more exciting and audacious styles of architecture and design in general. He worked on advanced architectural concepts. It looked like his future in architecture was inevitable, but it wasn't to be.

In the early 1990s the internet was becoming a world-wide phenomenon and just like the rest of the world, Dzudza was captivated by it. He left his hometown of Mostar (Yugoslavia, Bosnia and Herzegovina), which was known as one of the biggest landmarks and tourist attractions in all of Europe, and moved to the USA to continue his studies. Binghamton, N.Y., was his destination. "Binghamton University and the Binghamton community embraced me from the start and I felt very comfortable here," says Dzudza. While pursuing his degree in Graphic Design he continued to become more and more involved in expressing himself through the art of web design. He graduated Summa Cum Laude and moved to New York City where he worked at several .coms as a graphic designer, web developer, and creative director while absorbing new innovations and techniques in the fast changing web industry. In the late 1990s Dzudza founded Visible Motion Studios, a full media entertainment agency.

Dzudza's vision and interests have led him to work with variety of media. Today he has vast experience in the field of web and print design, e-commerce, flash architecture, TV, DVD design, video/audio integration, marketing, corporate identity design and image branding.

Suzanne M. Meredith
Writer

Suzanne Meredith has been capturing images with words for many years, but during the past two decades her publishing record has increased phenomenally. As an author, historian and journalist, juggling words has become a profession. She is the author and/or co-author of 13 books, with publishing contracts for several more volumes that are now in progress.

Meredith has received the Jefferson Award, with Ed Aswad, for exceptional service in the preservation and promotion of local history through the writing of photo/history books.

Over the years Meredith has produced hundreds of magazine and newspaper articles that have been printed in numerous prestigious publications. She is currently Town of Union Historian, a position she has held for ten years, and is a correspondent for the Gannett newspaper, the Press & Sun Bulletin.

This is her second year participating in *FACES of the Southern Tier* as contributing writer.

From the Creative Director

In the summer of 2005 Roger Brooks approached me with his idea of starting the FACES project and asked if I would collaborate in the creation of the book by taking on the role of Creative Director/Director of Photography. Listening to the story behind the book was incredible – the life story of his daughter Alexis, and learning about the roller-coaster ride the Brooks family has been on since the birth of Alexis and everything she has been through. There was not one doubt in my mind about doing the project - I immediately agreed. Alexis, a beautiful young girl, was inspiring and gave me additional motivation to work on the project and to make it the best. I was honored to be part of the FACES project. This was also an opportunity to increase public awareness of vascular birthmarks.

After the success of the 2006 book and tremendous support from the Southern Tier community, we were eager to start working on the 2007 edition. In the planning stages we were focused on a new and more exciting format for the book while keeping the successful concepts from the first edition. We liked the idea of staying with the black and white photos which give subjects unusual quality and display a classic fineness. Black and white photos are sophisticated and elegant. Their simplicity and uncluttered look give our subjects a polished, high-class feel. Without being distracted by color, viewers would be more focused on the subjects, recognizing their individuality and uniqueness.

Our team photographed subjects in the habitat where the story behind the photo would be told. Surrounding elements were carefully chosen to support the concept of the photo. The idea was to use a cohesive environment which would complement the subject. This was emphasized so nothing would dominate or distract from the main focus – the subject itself.

The inside of the book was designed to follow the overall concept of the first edition including easy-to-read verdana fonts, black and white graphics, and the official FACES logo and its variations. I introduced a new script signature font to give the pages a flowing, more relaxing tone which balances the other more hard-shaped elements. We dedicated full-page photos to each subject. I decided to stay with the simple and clean design so the photos and written parts would stand out.

Even though we kept the inside photos black and white I designed the book jacket in color to give it some freshness and to contrast the black and white photos found inside the book. Black as a background color in the jacket design was selected so the featured photos and other design elements would pop out at a glance.

The photo selection for the cover was a natural choice –a young lady whose inspiring story was the initial idea behind the FACES project, Alexis Brooks.

I am very proud of this edition. During a grueling and intense 2-month period we photographed and interviewed all 50 subjects, conceptualized and designed the book, and turned in the final project to the printers. Seeing the final product one month later was extremely satisfying. The biggest reward of the entire project was getting to know all 50 fascinating people by listening to their stories. We found ourselves in awe after interviews, looking at each other and thinking out loud, "Wow, what a story, would you ever think …"

In today's day and age where internet, TV and other means of media occupy our daily lives, we have less and less time to get to know our fellow citizens, neighbors, and community members. We at FACES Publications are making this small contribution to the Southern Tier community by providing a cross-sectional window of individuals who make our community so diverse and strong.

- Elsan Dzudza

FACES of the Southern Tier
2006 Honorees

Alex Alexander
Senator Warren Anderson
Fran Angeline
Francis & Helen Battisti
Ronald Benjamin
Anthony Brunelli
Jared Campbell
Eric Chen
Ryan Connolly
Nate Cortese
Kristine Cunningham
Lois DeFleur
Reverend Gary Doupe
Ed Folli
Scott Gallagher
Don Giovanni
Luigi Gobo
Bill Grace
Johnny Hart
Dr. Beverly Hosten
Phil Jordan
Bob Keller
Guido LeBron
Mark Levy
Senator Tom Libous
Floyd Maines
Tony Mitchell
Roger Neel
Albert Nocciolino
Jim Norris
Hidy Ochiai
Barbara Oldwine
Marla Olmstead
Jim Orband
Dave Pessagno
Nancy Phillips
Kathi Roberts
Dr. I.J. Rosefsky
David Rossi
Lana Rouff
Michael "Jingles" Rubino
Bernie Shifrin
Gerry Smith
Ray Stanton, II
Diane Stento
Pete Stewart
Joan Trepa
Mike Wales
Jackie Westcott
Kristina Wong

Visit Us Online

www.tierfaces.com

Do You Know a Face for FACES?

To receive more information on how you can get involved in *FACES*, or how you can bring *FACES* to your community, please call 607-723-0324, or visit www.tierfaces.com.